Mediation

By

Will Pryor
Mediation & Arbitration

WEST
ACADEMIC
PUBLISHING

Mat #41519447

Short and Happy Guide Series is a trademark registered in the U.S. Patent and Trademark Office.

© 2014 LEG, Inc. d/b/a West Academic

    444 Cedar Street, Suite 700
    St. Paul, MN 55101
    1-877-888-1330

Printed in the United States of America

ISBN: 978-0-314-28990-2

For the three women in my life . . . there are no words.

—Dad

Table of Contents

A Short & Happy Guide to Mediation

Introduction

I am a mediator and I love it. I spend my days going back and forth between parties to disputes, parties encamped in separate conference rooms. More often than not, the process results in resolution. What a funny thing to do!

Who Should Read This Book

If you regularly participate in mediations or just want to know more about the process and how it is practiced these days, this book may be useful.

If you are an individual or in a business and you may be headed to your first mediation in the near future, this book will certainly give you comfort and allow you to anticipate the opportunity and take advantage of it.

If you are a law student, and you have heard of "alternative dispute resolution" (often referred to as "ADR") and are wondering whether ADR is something you may want to take a professional interest in, read this book.

If you are a lawyer and want some ideas on how to use the mediation process more effectively for your clients, this book may help. Better yet, buy a big stack and hand out copies of this book to your clients to help them appreciate the path the two of you are headed down together!

Finally, if you are a mediator or thinking of becoming one, this book will have some suggestions for you that may improve your skills and make you a better mediator.

Everywhere, All the Time, and Why

If you are in business or a law practice, there is a better than even chance that you have participated in a mediation, or will someday soon. If you are a litigator or insurance adjuster, there is a better than even chance that you have been to dozens, or even hundreds of mediations. It sometimes seems that we have reached a state of "mediation everywhere, all the time".

There are abundant reasons for the explosive growth in the use of mediation. Our courts are increasingly irrelevant to more and more people, either because dockets are too crowded or legal services too expensive. Most people and businesses cannot afford the time and money it takes to obtain access to the "justice" dispensed by our courts. Some perceive our jury trial system to be the most inefficient dispute resolution mechanism ever invented. The jury trial, for many, represents failure, a breakdown in the way things ought to work. Not only do the wheels of justice turn slowly, and expensively, the verdicts of juries are inherently unpredictable and often less than satisfying. The perception that a jury verdict often results in something less than justice is increasingly common. At times we appear to worship at the altar of "the right to trial by jury," and yet most of the civilized world seems to get along just fine without juries. We routinely are reminded these days that juries have sent innocent defendants to prison, leaving us to wonder about the injustices handed out by our civil courts, as well.

Given these common experiences and perceptions, it is not surprising that an expensive, unpredictable and inefficient judicial system has provoked the widespread use of a simple and efficient alternative.

In this book I will try to explain the process of mediation, and how you can make the process work for you. We will discuss whether a dispute should be mediated and when, how to select a mediator best suited to a particular dispute, how to prepare for a mediation, things to do (and not do) during the process itself, and finally some concerns about how mediation is evolving and some things that need to be done to keep it on a positive, productive, and popular path.

Along the way I will share with you some stories, essays that try to capture some memorable moments in my mediation experience, but that also teach us important lessons.

So why do I love mediation?

I have been eyeball-to-eyeball with Dallas Cowboys, a country music star, a PGA Tour golfer, and a beautiful fashion model. I have beheld politicians, successful entrepreneurs, and a 19-year old, millionaire software designer. I have worked with widows who have lost hope, and parents who have lost children.

I have seen wives who cheated on their husbands. And I have seen a husband who cheated on his wife (his parents and sister were at the mediation of a business lawsuit filed by his mistress; his wife, at home, was not aware of our meeting that day to try to settle the dispute, *nor was she aware of the lawsuit, or even the affair!*)

I have seen a man with half of his face missing (it was burned off in a chainsaw accident in the piney woods of East Texas).

I have seen a doctor and the widow of the doctor's deceased patient come together to hug and cry on each others' shoulders; the doctor, sobbing, over and over, "I'm sorry, I am so sorry"; the widow suing him for his malpractice offering reassurance, over and over, "it's ok, it's ok".

I have been hit in the face with a wadded-up, written settlement offer made to the mother of a teenage boy killed in a tractor accident. The boy was her only child.

I have been subjected to a stream of profanity, unleashed on me—by a Dallas Cowboy.

Like most mediators, I love what I do. I work with other lawyers and their clients to resolve all kinds of disputes. Almost every day I meet new people, listen to their stories, and start down a path in search of a solution.

Putting aside for the moment a few concerns, I love mediation because it works, and because it has a funny way of helping people solve problems. This book will help you understand what mediation, in general, is all about and what your next mediation may hold in store. I hope this book will help you enjoy your next experience with mediation, and allow you to use it as effectively as possible to your benefit.

Look What It Done

"Is it my turn now?"

I knew we were in trouble.

The case was a dispute between an elderly, African-American woman (let's call her Judith), and the local county government (we'll call it The County) with whom she had been employed for over thirty years.

In the course of The County's "downsizing" and reorganization, Judith had been reassigned to a warehouse facility about twenty miles from her home. This move was not, she reasoned, the result of a rational, dispassionate plan, but obvious racial and gender discrimination, and in retaliation for her public protests at county government meetings on a wide range of issues for years.

The mediation was ordered by the court. Mediations often take place because a court orders the parties to do so. Once convened, though, the mediator retains a considerable amount of discretion as to how to direct the process. One of the most important decisions that the mediator faces at the outset is whether or not to convene a "joint session", a face-to-face meeting where the parties, usually through counsel, have a chance to summarize their perspectives. Joint sessions can be a critical part of the process. But in some circumstances they are to be avoided. In this case, I decided that the parties needed to address each other, but I could not have predicted what I was about to witness!

The lawyers on both sides had just completed their appropriate, if somewhat perfunctory, joint session presentations. I was halfway into my routine suggestion that we divide into separate caucuses, "Well, if no one has anything else . . .", when Judith turned to her lawyer and said: "Is it my turn now?"

Part of my job as the neutral facilitator, in a joint session, is to make sure there is not even the appearance of having "cut anyone off", so I quickly apologized and said, "Judith, please, if you would like to say something . . .".

Judith rose from her chair. In over 3,000 mediations, I don't believe I can recall another instance where someone, about to speak, got up out of their chair.

I sat, with everyone in the room, enraptured. For twenty minutes we were transfixed by the damndest soliloquy that any of us had ever heard. It started low, and it ended high. It started with a "day in the life" description of what catching a series of buses to get to the new facility meant to her day, to her grandchildren, and to her outlook on life, and near the end it included what "Martin" and "Rosa" would have wanted her to do.

It came from her heart. It was fantastic. And here's the best part.

We all sensed that Judith was winding down. But with a flourish Judith summoned the last of her remaining energy.

Claiming that the whole ordeal had caused her almost unbearable mental anguish, she cried, "And this is what it done to me!!!" Judith reached up, pulled her wig off to reveal a smooth palate of baldness, and threw the wig down on the conference table.

All of her hair had disappeared, the apparent result of the stress inflicted on Judith by the County.

Not all joint sessions are this dramatic. O.K., none of my joint sessions are this dramatic! But the anecdote contains important lessons.

Why did we have the joint session? Why did I let Judith go on and on? What was the value in allowing Judith the floor, for as long as she cared to speak?

The dispute could not have been resolved without Judith having a chance to speak, and others, including the mediator, having a chance to hear her story.

The County representatives experienced Judith's passion. Judith experienced an audience, her day in court.

One of the reasons why mediators tend to encourage joint sessions is the same reason lawyers often object to them: they are unscripted, they are dynamic, and occasionally that means that they are "out of control". Lawyers, because they like to control things and control their clients, are often uncomfortable with joint sessions, and encourage mediators to skip them. So while part of the mediator's task is to pay attention to a lawyer's suggestions, occasionally the mediator must exercise his or her discretion and bring the parties together, whether the lawyers like it or not. Lawyers don't know everything!

Mediation Summarized

First, a quick summary of the process most people refer to as "mediation".

Mediation, in the most informal sense, has been around for centuries. The village elder with no official title but the person everyone in the village would turn to when disagreements arose was a "mediator". Most office environments have someone who, because of her tenure, experience, interpersonal skills or wisdom, or a combination of all of these qualities, mediates conflicts about cubicle assignments, the rejection by the manager of a "jeans on Friday" proposal, and just about any other issue causing unrest in the office. Most churches have a "go-to" figure, who may or may not be the pastor or have any official title at all, when things get heated about whether the shutters in the sanctuary should be open or closed during the worship hour, or whether the floral display should be more prominently featured. Principals and assistant principals are mediators, intervening all day, every day in disputes between teachers and students, teachers and teachers, teachers and parents, or students and students. From the beginning of time conflicts have been mediated, and resolved, by neutral facilitators.

Years ago our oldest child was in kindergarten at the time I was just beginning my practice as a full-time, professional neutral. On the way home one afternoon, in her sweet little voice, she said, "Daddy, tell me again what it is you do?" I responded, "I am a mediator". "Oh yeah, you told me that before". We rode along in silence for a mile or so. "Daddy, tell me again. What does a mediator do?" "A mediator," I said, "helps people who are having an argument to work it out". "Oh yeah. You told me that before". Another mile or so of silence. "Daddy, you should come to my class. We have *lots* of arguments."

Intriguing as that level of disputing can certainly be at times, I have decided to write about a different level of dispute resolution, the mediation of disputes where litigation of the dispute is pending, or litigation is threatened.

"Mediation" in this book is an informal, off-the-record negotiation facilitated by a neutral third-party, the mediator. It is usually referred to as "non-binding," which means that, if the process is unsuccessful, the result is an impasse and the parties are right where they were before. The parties have no obligation to reach an agreement, and the mediator cannot order or direct the outcome. In most jurisdictions, all communication throughout the process is confidential, and not to be used again later for any purpose.

"Non-binding" does *not* mean that, if the process results in a signed, written settlement agreement, the agreement is not binding and enforceable. To the contrary, a signed, written mediated settlement agreement ("MSA") is as binding and enforceable as any other contract.

Mediation is not "arbitration." In arbitration the neutral is a private judge, hired and paid by the parties to render a decision which, like a court order or judgment, is final and binding on the parties.

In the type of mediation discussed in this book the parties are typically represented by counsel and the mediator is usually compensated evenly by the parties. The process begins with an agreement regarding the choice of the mediator, and a date, place and time for the meeting. It is typical of the process in most jurisdictions that the lawyers communicate with the mediator by phone, in person, or in writing in advance of the mediation session, to prepare the mediator for the main event. It is to everyone's advantage that the mediator have a chance to anticipate the nature of the dispute, to consider what key factual and legal issues might be involved, and in general to have a sense of the dynamics of the dispute (personalities, prior settlement negotiations, etc.).

Rules in a Knife Fight?

In Butch Cassidy and the Sundance Kid, there is a famous scene in which Butch (Paul Newman) gets himself in a tough spot. Butch has been challenged to a knife fight, to the death, for control of the gang, by a menacing and physically superior enemy. As Butch is about to be sliced into small pieces Butch suddenly and innocently announces that they must first have a meeting of the minds as to the rules to be observed, and heads towards his opponent as if they are about to have a conversation. Bad Guy: "Rules? Butch, we don't need rules in a knife fi . . ." Before the last word can be uttered, Butch unexpectedly and violently administers a swift kick to the manhood area of the Bad Guy, causing the Bad Guy to crumple to the ground. Game. Set. Match. Butch walks away the winner.

Mediation should in no way resemble a knife fight, but like a knife fight, mediation does not require many rules! Efforts from time to time to layer rules on the process (more stringent requirements on mediator qualifications, more formal reporting requirements on mediators in court-appointed cases, etc.) are almost always turned away. There is beauty in the simplicity of mediation. [The prevailing wisdom has long been that the less structure that is imposed on the process, the more popular and effective it will become.] Even as the practice of mediation becomes commercial, most feel that it would be unwise to stray too far away from its roots in the "village elder" model of dispute resolution.

But mediations often have a general overlay of rules or guidelines authored by statute, the local courts, a state supreme court, or a neutral service-providing organization, such as the American Arbitration Association ("AAA"), Judicial Arbitration & Mediation Services ("JAMS"), the International Center for Conflict Prevention & Resolution ("CPR"), and others.

The "rules" tend to follow this outline:

Qualifications of the Mediator: The mediator is obligated to be neutral: the mediator should certainly not have a financial interest in the matter being mediated, should not have a relationship with any of the parties or counsel that would create a conflict of interest, should disclose any circumstance that might give rise to a conflict or even the appearance of a conflict, and should refrain from serving as mediator of any matter in which he or she does not feel competent or qualified to serve.

Authority of the Mediator: Discretion in facilitating the process is granted to the mediator: the mediator can convene the parties, or not, can suggest appropriate steps to follow throughout the process, and can declare a recess or impasse at any time.

Limitations on the Authority of the Mediator: Most sets of rules make it clear that the mediator does not have the authority to require the parties to agree; the authority of the parties to reach an agreement rests solely with the parties; the mediator is not a decision-maker, and lacks the authority of an arbitrator.

Confidentiality: Most rules make it clear that the process is private and confidential; only parties, their representatives, and counsel, may participate, absent an agreement to the contrary; the mediator is typically prohibited from disclosing to anyone, including an appointing court, anything about what transpires at the mediation, other than the matter was resolved, reached an impasse, or was recessed; the participants are assured, by this rule, that nothing they say or do in the process of mediating can be used again later for any purpose. If one party should make a statement during the mediation, opposing counsel may not, months later when that party is in a deposition or on the witness stand, be cross-examined on the statement: "Isn't it true that back in June at the mediation you acknowledged that you were sorry for your conduct towards my client?" This blanket confidentiality is frustrating, at times, to a party who feels that their participation in the process was exemplary, and their adversary's involvement comtemptable. Mediators are sometime requested or implored by one party to report the other party's "bad behavior" to the Court. But in most instances the mediator will decline. The mediator may usually disclose that one side failed to appear, or failed to pay their share of the mediator's fee, but if they appear and pay their share of the fee, in theory they may sit mute with their arms crossed, or dance on the conference tables, without consequence.

Authority of the parties: Named parties in lawsuits or individual parties to a dispute are usually obligated to personally appear and participate in a mediation; this is the easy part of a participation rule; the hard part is what to do about participation of corporations, businesses, partnerships, governmental bodies, and other entities. "Party representatives must have full authority to settle" and "all persons necessary to the decision to settle shall be present," are typical of participation rules. But compliance with this rule often ranges from challenging, to unrealistic, to impossible. Try scheduling a mediation where the presence of an entire Board of Directors or Board of Trustees is required! And in a governmental setting, a claim involving a municipality, a county, a school district, or other agency, literal compliance with a participation rule, in a process which is confidential, would place the governmental entity squarely in conflict with an applicable open meetings statute. In practice, an entity's compliance with a participation rule will ultimately require trusting the entity to participate in good faith. Is the participation requirement occasionally manipulated, creating a problem for the mediator and impairing the process? Certainly (see Chapters 4 and 7), but for the most part the rule is effective in reminding parties of their obligations to the process.

Date, time and place? Harder than you thought!: The authority of the mediator generally includes final say as to the date, time and location of the mediation. When a mediation is taking place by an agreement of the parties, obviously the agreement should include a date, a time, and a locale. But these issues can get tricky in the context of a court-ordered mediation. Assume the court's scheduling order requires the dispute to be mediated no later than 30 days before the trial setting, but the trial setting is 18 months away. The Plaintiff contacts you, the mediator, and says, "we see no need for a lot of discovery, please schedule the mediation in the next 30 days". The Defendant responds to this suggestion by saying, "there is no way we can evaluate the case without discovery, so please wait at least six months and perhaps a year before contacting us again about scheduling." What should you do? Following either directive will be seen by one party as the mediator's "taking sides." Choosing the mid-point will make both parties unhappy.

Let's say the parties agree on the date for the mediation, but the Plaintiff prefers a "full day" mediation beginning at 8:30 am, but the Defendant insists on a "half day" and wants to start at 1:30 pm? Or the parties agree on a date and on a "half day," but the Plaintiff wants the morning, and the Defendant wants the afternoon? What do you, the mediator, do? Good question!

The location of the mediation can also become an issue. Many mediators have their own offices and conference rooms, and host most of the mediations they conduct. But some mediators are retired judges, or retired lawyers, or do business from a home office. What then? In some instances the mediator will ask if one side or the other would be willing to host the mediation. If this is not objected to, there is usually no problem with such an arrangement. But there are circumstances when a "neutral location" is deemed essential. Then the mediator may elect to find a hotel with conference rooms or an executive suite in an office building with daily-rental conference rooms; in addition, the parties might use the local courthouse, or a neutral law firm's offices.

To many the issue of a "neutral location" may seem silly, but put a neutral site on the list of conditions that participants may have. Years ago I was asked to travel to Chicago to mediate a dispute. Both parties were represented by large law firms, one in Chicago and one in Cleveland. And though the Cleveland lawyers acquiesced and agreed that the mediation could take place in Chicago, they were unwilling to agree to allow the Chicago lawyers to host the gathering at their offices in Chicago. So I was tasked with finding suitable conference facilities at a major, downtown Chicago hotel. This was a three-day mediation, and the cost of reserving these conference facilities, shared evenly by the parties, was not incidental.

Why the paranoia about a neutral site? Who knows! Sometimes control of the facilities strikes some as equal to control of the process. If one law firm is hosting the mediation, is it more likely that the draft settlement documents will be generated on conveniently available computers by conveniently available support staff? Are there other amenities, or resources, that will inevitably be made available to the hosts, and not the guests?

No Court Reporter / No Processor Servers: Many sets of mediation rules will include a prohibition that no participant be served with "process" (a/k/a suit papers, subpoenas, etc.) at the mediation. The gathering is, of course, supposed to be a settlement discussion, not a means of perpetuating conflict. And as if it weren't obvious in connection with an informal, private, and confidential discussion, no recording of the event is permitted.

Mediation fees: The mediator's fees, if any, are almost always divided evenly by the parties. Occasionally the parties will agree that one side will pay the entire fee, and this is normally acceptable. It is worth noting, however, that if you cheerfully accept the offer of your opponent to pay the full fee, the mediation may have a funny way of becoming *their* mediation. Think of it this way: when two people go to an expensive restaurant on their first date, and one of them picks up the check at the end of the meal, there is no unwritten obligation of the other, no strings attached. Or is there?

What if one side can afford to pay its share of the mediation fee, but the other side can't? When a mediation is court-ordered, and I learn that one side is *pro se* (i.e. unrepresented by counsel), it is my practice to offer to conduct the mediation and waive the *pro se's* share of the fee. My view is that a party is usually unrepresented because they can't afford to pay a lawyer. I am serving the Court, as well as the parties, and I don't want my fee to become a problem that the Court has to solve. But even when I volunteer to waive one party's share of the fee, I won't do so unless the other party, the party paying a share of the fee, agrees. Why not? Let's say the Plaintiff is trying to collect money owed by the Defendant. The Defendant is *pro se*, but the Plaintiff believes that the Defendant has plenty of money and is just being evasive. The Plaintiff may want the mediation to occur because it will force the Defendant to sit at a negotiation table and incur the time and expense that goes along with the process. Making the Defendant write a check to the mediator may be an important goal of the Plaintiff. Perhaps to avoid paying the mediator, the deadbeat Defendant will actually offer the Plaintiff, prior to the mediation, some of the amount owed! If I were to unilaterally agree to waive the fee, the Plaintiff may be justifiably upset.

More than once in my mediation experience I have agreed to waive or reduce my fee for a party who claimed poverty. When the mediation revealed that the party actually had significant resources, and agreed to pay, or worse receive, real money to settle the dispute, guess who was justifiably upset!

All Together Now (Part I)

In the classic model of the process, the mediator brings all participants together at the outset for a "joint session". Joint sessions will be part of the discussion elsewhere in this book. The mediator makes a few comments, goes over the ground rules, answers any questions that the participants have, and attempts to create an atmosphere conducive to negotiation and compromise. Next, each side, usually through the lawyer, has an opportunity while everyone is still assembled to summarize their position and perspectives on the issues in dispute. These presentations are often perfunctory ("we are here in good faith to try to settle this case"), but in some cases the presentations are elaborate, and will include PowerPoint presentations, videotape of witness testimony, tabbed, three-ring notebooks, and other handouts. Many of the anecdotes in this book are from memorable joint sessions.

When the joint session has run its course, the parties retire to separate conference rooms, sometimes referred to as "private caucuses." Often the rest of the process consists of nothing more than the mediator going back and forth, encouraging proposals and counter-proposals until, hopefully, the matter is resolved.

An Ahhhh Moment

Remember when you were a kid and you got home from church or synagogue and you finally could put on your cool and comfortable play outfit to replace the hot and itchy dress clothes you had been in for several hours, and you could get a cold drink and you were finally free and unrestrained and you could run around and not be forced to sit quietly, and stoically, with *adults*? It was awesome!

I think that the moment the joint session is adjourned, and the parties are allowed to retreat to their separate rooms, is one of every participant's favorite moments in the entire mediation process. They can finally put on their play clothes. It should not be overlooked that for many participants, mediation may be a special moment in their lives, a unique and important experience, an event where the only lawsuit they will ever be a party to may be resolved, or not resolved. The dispute may have been causing tremendous strain on their family, or business, or both, for a year or longer. And the mediation may be the first moment in the vast span of the dispute to confront the enemy, the individual or entity who has been causing the strain, the frustration, and the high blood pressure. Mediators should be mindful of this. For those of us who engage in the process professionally, whether as advocates, as client representatives, or as neutrals, I believe that too often a mechanical or routinized approach to the process may be the result of our experience. This is natural and to be expected. Any human endeavor that we engage in repetitively may be something that at some point becomes routine, reflexive, a matter of "muscle memory." But those of us engaged in the process professionally should always remember that there may be other participants in the process for whom this is a special day, and the joint session perhaps a special moment, one long anticipated.

So the long anticipated day arrived, all of the preparation completed, and the confrontation is now over. The parties who have been at war with each other for a year or two have sat across the table from each other and survived the ordeal. It is time to remove the jacket, to relax, grab a soft drink, and tell the mediator what they *really* think!

The mediator is the only participant in the process who gets to be "in both rooms." It is in a private caucus that a disputant can unload and download her concerns, fears, anger, and argument. The "private caucus" is a chance for each party to talk about the other, and few fail to take full advantage. While the entire mediation process is usually "confidential," a private caucus communication can be "super-confidential," meaning a party can share information with the mediator and instruct the mediator not to raise the issue with the adversary. It is in the private caucus that the mediator becomes a listener, a teacher, a juror, and sometimes a friend.

One for You, One for Me

Many mediations involve a "negotiation dance," the back and forth negotiation initiated by a ridiculously high demand, and countered by an equally absurd low-ball offer. There is a reason for this. Regrettably, the "high demand / low offer" technique has been proven in numerous negotiation studies to be the negotiation technique most likely to lead to resolution of a dispute. Perhaps counter-intuitively for some, the technique least likely to produce an agreement is where one party "plants his flag," taking a bottom line position from the outset and challenging the other side to eventually acquiesce to it. Kids, don't try this at home! It's dangerous!

Often a mediation turns into a back and forth process until, hopefully, the matter is resolved. The parties are engaged, essentially, in "positional" or "competitive" bargaining, but as will be explained in this book, the mediator is constantly engaged in "interest based" negotiation. It is this unique perspective of the mediator that often resolves disputes that were otherwise incapable of resolution.

Can You Keep a Secret?

Of all the rules mentioned thus far, the only one of practical application is the one that generally guarantees the confidentiality of all communication throughout the process. Rules pertaining to confidentiality may vary a bit from jurisdiction to jurisdiction, but as a general proposition, everything the participants share with the mediator, and everything they share with each other, is not to be used again later for any purpose. This confidentiality cloak is a key feature of mediation. The veil is never to be lifted. In most jurisdictions mediators are prohibited, by statute or by court rules, from ever disclosing anything about the mediation process to a court (or anyone else), other than that the matter was resolved, or that the process concluded in an impasse. Strict confidentiality is why, in this book, names of the participants are changed, and other facts in the stories tweaked to disguise real cases.

The process is dynamic; it is not scripted. Although the classic model is as just described, it is not unusual at some point during the process for the mediator to have a conversation with only the attorneys. In some cases, when it makes sense, usually in a matter where the parties to the dispute were previously in some form of relationship, the lawyers are excused from the process and the mediator facilitates a "clients-only" meeting. In other words, most mediators subscribe to a "whatever works" philosophy. The challenge for the mediator is to facilitate communication by the best means available, and the best means available will always depend on the personalities of and roles being played by each participant. The hope, of course, is that the communication will lead to a better understanding by each side of the other's position and, eventually, compromise and resolution.

How Does a Mediation Get Started?

A mediation occurs for one of three reasons.

First, over the last twenty to thirty years, courts all over the United States have been ordering more and more cases to mediation. Over-crowded courts can become dependent on aggressive mediation referrals for docket control, and court-ordered mediation is often a condition of being allowed to proceed to trial. The court referral of pending cases is how the current use of mediation got started, and how many mediators gained their early experience. In my personal experience, the first several hundred mediations I conducted were all court-ordered, and I was chosen by the court and imposed on the parties as the mediator. In recent years most court referral programs have evolved to where the parties are ordered to mediate as a condition of being allowed to proceed to trial, but the court gives the parties flexibility as to the timing of the mediation and the selection of a neutral.

Other disputes end up being mediated, not because of a court order, but because the dispute arises out of a contract between the parties, and the contract has a provision that requires that the parties mediate as a condition of one party's filing a lawsuit, or proceeding to binding arbitration. Mediation clauses were virtually non-existent as recently as the 1970s. Now these clauses are common. Contracts pertaining to construction, lending, insurance, investments, employment, and even consumer/manufacturer or consumer/retailer relationships frequently have a mediation provision. Contractual mediation clauses will continue to fuel the use of mediation for decades to come.

Finally, many mediations take place with no court order, and with no pre-dispute contractual mediation clause. In my view, this is an extremely positive development. More and more often, institutional litigants such as banks, financial services companies, insurance companies, and employers proceed to mediation either because they have experienced success with an aggressive mediation program, or because of a pervasive feeling that "well, a court is going to force us to mediate anyway, so we might as well try it before we spend a lot of money on lawyers." More and more often parties are simply agreeing to mediate.

Who Gets to Be the Mediator?

Anyone can be a mediator. In my state we have a statute that requires a person to attend a forty-hour mediator training course to be eligible to receive a court-referred mediation. But there is no license or certification exam, and no such training is required for mediations that take place by agreement, or when the parties have selected any mediator they desire. There is no age requirement in the statute, or a requirement of a law degree or even a college degree! The market for neutral services is a market in which there are virtually no barriers to entry. Want to be a mediator? Congratulations, you are one!

But most mediators are lawyers. Mediators are often former judges, or at least they have years of experience that imparts an aura of wisdom and credibility. Regardless of their qualifications or credentials, mediators tend to be personable and outgoing, and they tend to derive satisfaction from helping other people work through and resolve their disputes.

In some types of cases, especially family law matters, non-lawyer mediators are common.

More often than not the process is ultimately helpful to both sides. In the process of shuttling back and forth, the mediator nudges and encourages the parties to offer settlement proposals and to counter proposals from the other side. When successful, the mediator reveals that an agreement has been achieved. When not successful, an impasse is declared and the parties go forward with their dispute. But even when an impasse is the result, it is not uncommon for some or all of the participants to conclude that the process was worth the time, effort and money expended on it. Nor is it uncommon for a case that reached an impasse at mediation to settle the next day, or next week, or following month, when resolution probably could not have been achieved without the communication that was shared at the mediation.

Mediation works, and that's why it's not going away.

The Music Star

It is a tale as old as time. The talented musician hires an agent. While the artist is waiting tables, mowing lawns, and waiting for the "big break", the agent's percentage of the earnings is pretty much "who cares". But finally the big break happens, and the artist becomes an overnight sensation. The hits, packed arenas, and movie roles follow. Money, the root of all evil and most lawsuits, starts rolling in.

"Wait a minute, why am I paying that big percentage of my income to my agent? My fans aren't paying to see HIM!" So the agent is fired. A lawsuit is filed. Mediation ensues.

At the mediation all the parties were, to say the least, well represented. Entertainment law is one of the sexiest practices in the legal profession, and it tends to attract fine lawyers. Those who are really exceptional get to represent the top performers, and the agents who sue them.

One of the lawyers happened to be a good friend of mine. Susan is a good lawyer, she explained to me that she thought a joint session would be very valuable, and she had prepared a presentation. Taking the time to anticipate an opportunity to present a summary of a case directly, face-to-face, to the other side in a joint session, is something that good lawyers do. The joint session, and the opportunity it gives a lawyer to provide unfiltered communication to the opposing party, is often critically important to getting the case resolved. The way the rules work in our courts, lawyers are prohibited from communicating directly with the party on the other side at every phase of a lawsuit. It would be exceedingly unprofessional, and worse, for a lawyer to call the client on the other side during the pendency of litigation. All communication by a lawyer during the litigation must be through opposing counsel, and sometimes the biggest obstacle to resolution of a lawsuit is either the actual ineffectiveness of opposing counsel acting as a filter of all communication to his or her client, or even just the concern that the client is only receiving a version of the communication that opposing counsel wants.

In any event, at this mediation and in this joint session, Susan, representing the agent, was delivering her version of "the truth" directly to the musician, and it was working.

But I had already greased the skids.

As both sides and their representatives and attorneys were assembling in a conference room for the joint session (there were about fifteen people present), I started in with a comment or two, as I will often do, just to break the ice and put everyone at ease.

"First, I feel I must disclose this morning that I have never listened to your music, Mr. Talent. But, who would have guessed, as I was leaving my house this morning I mentioned to Ellen, my wife, what case I was mediating today. And she said, 'oh my God, he's fabulous.' I had no idea, Mr. Talent, but my wife is a big fan of yours."

My comment produced the desired chuckle from all around the conference table, helping everyone relax. The artist swelled with pride. "Will, that's o.k. Tell Ellen that I appreciate her support." Everyone laughed some more.

I had appealed to the ego of a talented artist. It turned out to be helpful.

More importantly, everyone was at ease in what otherwise might have started out as a tense discussion. We were off and running.

The day wore on. Into the evening. Back and forth. Finally, as often happens, the parties achieved a compromise.

Susan was packing her files and materials. I offered to help her get her boxes together, as everyone else had already headed out into the evening.

"Will, thanks. You did a great job today. We didn't really think it could be settled, but you helped a lot."

"Susan, I always feel like mediators get too much credit when cases settle, and too much blame when they don't!"

"Well, you can think that if you want. But we appreciate your efforts."

And then this. "By the way, Will, that was amazing that it turns out that Ellen is a big fan [of Mr. Talent]."

And my response. "Susan, that 'going out the door' conversation with Ellen this morning? Ellen's out of town. That conversation never happened."

There was a long pause. It took my friend a few seconds to appreciate what I had just shared with her.

Whenever you are dealing with a celebrity, a musician, an artist, an author, an athlete, or a politician of any note, there is a reasonably good chance that he or she will have a larger than normal ego, and I have learned that it is not all that difficult to appeal to that ego.

Appealing to the ego of anyone, even a non-celebrity, is important. Acknowledging, or even complimenting, directly or indirectly, someone else's achievement, or stature, is a quick and simple way of telling them, "I get it. I get you. I recognize who I am dealing with here."

By making up the story I told in the joint session, did I do wrong?

Mediation provides an opportunity for the parties to a dispute to come together and, in a focused environment, to attempt to resolve the dispute. The mediator's task, sometimes, is to create that environment. I am not suggesting that mediators should lie without shame in order to facilitate compromise and resolution. But I do believe that mediators have license to assist, to nudge, to encourage, and sometimes to grease the skids of discourse.

CHAPTER 2

Should You Mediate, and When?

For as long as I can remember lawyers and judges have considered the following statement axiomatic: 95% (or so) of all lawsuits that get filed never go to trial. Most disputes are dismissed for lack of pursuit, dismissed for a legal infirmity, or settled. For whatever reason, for decades a tiny fraction of disputes went the distance.

So now that mediation is all the rage? Now that courts all across the country are referring cases to mediators, sometimes multiple referrals of the same case? You may have seen this coming: 95% (or so) of all filed lawsuits never go to trial! In other words, nothing has changed! Most cases are still dismissed or settled.

So what's the big deal? Why not let nature take its course? Why shell out extra money for a fancy mediator and incur additional delay by scheduling and then conducting a mediation when a dispute is likely to be resolved the old fashioned way; that is, without mediation? Many old school lawyers will tell you that the widespread use of mediation has had a chilling effect on the kinds of settlement conversations that lawyers used to have "back in the day." Too often, they will tell you, the inevitable mediation will actually forestall and delay a conversation that years ago might have led to settlement. How ironic. To answer these questions, let's begin by asking two more questions: should a dispute be mediated, and if so, when?

Should you mediate your dispute? At the risk of appearing to be doing nothing but posing an endless series of questions, we have to ask one more! The first consideration in answering the "should you mediate" question has to always be: *do you want the matter resolved?* Believe it or not, the answer to this question is not always "of course."

Compelling

There are a variety of reasons why people sometimes do not want their dispute to be compromised and settled. I mediated a case a few years ago involving a widow suing her husband's surgeon, alleging that the surgeon's negligence caused her husband's death. Late in the day she said very kindly, "Will, I appreciate what you are trying to do, but I do not want to settle my case. If I settle, it will mean that I accept money from his (the doctor's) insurance carrier, I will be required to sign a release and probably a confidentiality agreement, and this lawsuit will be of no consequence." She continued, "If they offered me a *billion dollars* I wouldn't take it. I want my case to go to trial so that the public can be educated about what happened, so that his reputation is ruined to the point that he can never practice medicine again, and so that he can never do what he did to my husband to anyone ever again."

As it turned out, the doctor she was suing had been sued a number of times, and for whatever reason, he had bounced around from state to state, and hospital to hospital, miraculously maintaining his license and staff privileges in the face of evidence of a chemical dependency. The widow wanted to put a stop to it.

It is important to acknowledge the goals of disputing parties that sometimes have nothing to do with monetary compensation. It is often said, "It's not about the money." Cynics will roll their eyes and point out that usually, when all is said and done, it's all about the money! There is some basis for such cynicism. But sometimes it turns out that the dispute really was about something else. The widow wanted justice. She also wanted to perform a public service. And the widow was correct that none of her goals in the matter would be accomplished by compromising and settling.

The widow's case for pursuing a public trial was compelling. Our courts exist for a reason and the reason, presumably, is so that justice may be done.

Not as Compelling

But there are other cases in which the pursuit of justice may be a stated goal, but the explanation is less compelling. In an employment case, the mistreated former employee bringing a claim against the former employer, an employer who had the temerity to pass them over for a promotion(!), will often assume the position of a rebel fighting for the cause of justice on behalf of all of the other mistreated souls, both past and future, back at the shop. But in many cases the evidence of the basis for the adverse employment decision may be a mixed bag, as easily explained by a legitimate business practice, or the dubious performance of the employee, as by an improper and illegal motive.

The mediator in such an instance should listen to the employee and acknowledge his or her emotions. How they feel, after all, is how they feel. Self-righteous indignation, even when misplaced, is still self-righteous indignation! But having acknowledged the feelings that underlie the claim, the mediator should also do a reality check with the employee, to make sure the employee has a grasp on the likelihood of ultimately prevailing. Mediator: "Is there a theoretical possibility that the goals you are pursuing might be achieved at the courthouse? Of course, but let's be realistic. If you tried your case to ten different juries, how often do you think you would win?"

Not Compelling

So there is the goal of pursuing justice, whatever that may mean, and then there is the occasional recreational litigant, the person with a sporting view of disputing. These are people who are "in it to win it." They want to screw their adversary. They want to win, and if along the way they can ruin their opponent's business, marriage, and reputation, so much the better!

A long time ago I mediated a case involving the largest individual customer of a major brokerage firm in my hometown. This investor had a huge stake in a futures market. One day this market went into freefall. The brokerage firm began to frantically call and fax the customer (this occurred before the invention of the internet and email) to obtain his instructions and authorization as to how to proceed. The customer failed to respond. By the end of the day the firm's failed attempted contacts had become margin calls and under the agreements between the broker and customer, several other of his accounts had been liquidated to cover his margin. The brokerage firm sued the customer (he owed the firm money), and the customer sued the firm (for breaching fiduciary duties—he was dyslexic and alleged that the firm knew it, and knew he couldn't read the faxes throughout the day).

"Will," the customer told me around 6:00 p.m., after a long day that had produced no progress, with each side still making dollar demands on the other, "You've told me that I only have about a one-in-ten chance of prevailing, and that's what my lawyers are telling me." He continued, "You've also suggested that it might cost me another $200,000 or $300,000 in attorney's fees to continue to pursue this, and my lawyers agree with that, as well." And then this, "But all of you also agree that if I win, I will get *millions.*" Long pause. "I like it."

In that moment I realized that I was dealing with a professional risk-taker, a man who understood risk and appreciated it, a man who invested in high-risk, high-return investments because he was good at it and enjoyed it. The lawsuit was just another investment. This litigant knew how to perform a risk-reward analysis. To him the choice was clear.

And in case I had missed the point, on his way out he thanked me for my efforts and said, "one more thing . . . I want a piece of their ass."

The investor epitomized the recreational and the sporting disputant, someone with money and ego who can't be persuaded that he should consider settling his case.

So if it's "justice," however you define it, you are after, or if settlement is not a goal, then don't mediate.

Normal? Who's Normal?

But let's talk about normal people. Normal people do not have a desire to be a party to a dispute. Normal people do not enjoy risk, spending money on lawyers and expert witnesses and court reporters, and spending their time hunting down documents their lawyer says have to be copied and produced for the other side. Normal people do not enjoy sitting for a deposition. Normal people do not enjoy going to the courthouse, whether it's for jury duty or because they are a party to a lawsuit.

Once the threshold decision has been made regarding preferring to settle versus not settle, there remain questions about whether mediation is a suitable option, about timing and appropriate next steps.

Does it depend on the type of case? Do construction disputes settle more often than employment cases? Do collection cases settle with a higher frequency than landlord-tenant disputes? As a general proposition there is very little empirical evidence that the type of case makes a great deal of difference in settlement rates.

Does the cost of disputing outweigh the potential benefit? Let's say you are trying to collect a debt of $2,500, and you are in a state that doesn't allow you to collect the attorney's fees you will incur in your collection effort. It won't take long for your pursuit of the claim to lack economic viability. In other words, if a prompt and efficient settlement cannot be reached, it will never make economic sense to pursue the claim. An early mediation might be helpful.

Is there any prospect of an ongoing relationship between the parties? Occasionally a business dispute has the potential for a creative solution, perhaps one involving future business consideration. A facilitated negotiation may be the best process available for salvaging a win-win solution.

Is there a risk of a trade secret, proprietary information, or other matters best kept confidential being disclosed in discovery or in a public courtroom? Mediation is a confidential process, and mediated settlement agreements often include an agreement between the parties regarding confidentiality. If you have information worth protecting, mediation may provide a solution.

Is time of the essence? The old-fashioned way of negotiating settlements often meant waiting until the case was on the eve of trial, on the "courthouse steps." Time is money. Months of litigation discovery is expensive, distracting, stressful, and often unnecessary for proper risk evaluation. Often there are business or personal considerations that make unnecessary delay problematic.

Do you have enough information about your side of the case, and your opponent's, to perform an appropriate evaluation of your interests and your options? This one is tricky. An increasing number of mediations are being conducted "pre-suit," either because of a contractual obligation to mediate or due to one or more of the foregoing considerations, which must be balanced. Early mediations provide an opportunity to achieve great efficiency. On the other hand, lawyers are often queasy at the prospect of having to advise a client regarding a potential settlement until they have done enough discovery to evaluate the likeliest litigation scenarios and outcomes. Whether to engage in an early mediation is often a coin toss. There are advantages and disadvantages of going in either direction. But practically and relatively, attempting an early mediation has little potential downside.

The Good Faith / Bad Faith Thing: Will Your Opponent Engage In An Honest Negotiation? The challenge on this one is that it is a consideration beyond your control. Your answer will require speculation. But it is an important consideration nonetheless, because if you are certain that your opponent will be unable or unwilling to engage in a meaningful negotiation, then it would be illogical to mediate.

There are certain types of cases in which your opponent might be unable to negotiate. A collection case where the borrower is penniless is an example, as well as a case where the dispute involves someone who has outstanding bank loans, and the loan documents say that agreeing to some forms of settlement would be an "event of default."

But a larger category of cases includes those in which one party might be able but is simply unwilling to negotiate, as discussed earlier in this chapter (the recreational / sporting disputant). This is an area in which the expressions "good faith" and "bad faith" are often raised. "Will the other side participate in good faith?" "The offer they are making is an insult; they're here in bad faith." More often than not the discussion of good faith vs. bad faith gives me an ice cream headache! But the use of these expressions in the context of mediation is common enough that we must discuss it.

In my experience, if Sally accuses Fred of bad faith, this actually means that Sally disagrees with Fred and is upset about it. But I will acknowledge that whatever bad faith is, it happens.

My favorite example of bad faith is what I refer to as "purposeful under-participation." In a later chapter we will discuss the importance of the physical presence at the mediation of decision-makers, as opposed to allowing participation by phone, and how participation considerations should always be a part of your preparation for a mediation. But here purposeful participation occurs when one side sends the "wrong person" to the mediation *on purpose*, to gain leverage in the negotiation.

An analysis of good faith can begin with consideration of whether the participation by one party, the insurer, *complies with a court order*. If an insurance policy provides for $1 million in liability coverage, but the personal injury claimant has medical expenses of only $10,000 and has lost no time from work, has the insurer satisfied a court's mediation order that it have someone present at the mediation with "full authority" if its claim representative attending the mediation has authority to settle for an amount up to $25,000? Probably. Is there a different answer if his or her authority is up to $50,000? Not really. Presuming an internal, objective evaluation by the insurer concluded that the claim had a settlement value of less than $25,000, or less than $50,000, then the insurer had a representative with "authority" present at the mediation. We do not, and should not, require insurance companies to send representatives to mediations with check writing authority to the limit of the policy in every case.

But here's the problem. At the end of the eight-hour mediation, after all of the attendees have participated in information gathering and reevaluation, and have shared in the tedium, frustration and boredom of a very long and exhausting negotiation process, the mediator suggests that the claim be settled for $60,000. All participants, including the claim representative in attendance, agree that this is a reasonable suggestion. However, the claim representative must call his or her supervisor for the additional authority necessary to resolve the claim. The supervisor, whose focus and energies have been directed throughout the eight-hour mediation on other matters, declines to approve the additional authority. Or worse, it's after 5:00 pm and the supervisor is no longer answering the phone! The mediator, reluctantly, declares an impasse. Regrettably, the participants leave the mediation certain that, had the supervisor been physically present, the matter would have been compromised and settled. Physical participation matters.

Has the insurer participated in the mediation in bad faith? Maybe. Again, it depends on the internal, objective evaluation performed by the insurer. If a good faith, objective evaluation of the claim is $25,000, then sending a claims representative with authority to settle for up to $50,000 could hardly be described as bad faith. If the insurer's objective evaluation, however, is that the claim has a value up to $50,000, *and the insurer intentionally* *sends a representative with authority to settle for up to $25,000,* then the insurer is arguably violating at least the spirit of the court order, and certainly is threatening the credibility of a process which depends, in part, on collaborative, problem solving participation by all interested parties. Purposeful under-participation, in my experience, is a demonstration of bad faith, as much as I hate the term!

Another example is the lawyer who is called to trial, is un-prepared, and begs the court for a continuance by stating, "Your Honor, if you will grant a continuance and order us back to mediation, I promise that my client will make a good faith effort to settle the case"; mediation then occurs a couple of weeks later and the client appears and makes no offer of settlement. Bad faith? I rest my case!

There will be a lengthy discussion of some of the "ills" of the current practice of mediation in the final chapter of this book. But as counter-intuitive as it may seem to many, the remedy of legislating or ordering good faith in the mediation process is not an obvious solution. Many ADR practitioners and courts, while frustrated at the occasional misuse of the process, have concluded that a good faith prescription would be worse than the illness, and have declined to inquire into the quality of the ordered participation. Other than ordering participation and payment of a share of the mediation fee, most courts are reluctant to go further. But whether you can count on your adversary to participate in a mediation in "good faith" (yuk, I said it again), must be a consideration when deciding whether to go forward with a mediation.

Illustrating the advantage of an early mediation, one where the need for confidentiality was paramount, is the following mediation from years ago.

The New Hire

She was really pretty. Really, really pretty. Lisa was the newly hired Director of Development for a highly regarded private school, and she arrived on the job with impeccable credentials and an impressive fundraising track record. The trustees of the school had had to reach to accommodate her compensation requirements, but no one thought she would not be worth every penny.

Chet was the hard-charging and highly regarded Principal of the school. Chet had been at his post for five years when Lisa appeared on the scene, and the school's reputation continued to rise throughout his tenure. Chet was accessible to faculty and parents, and the students thought he had a "cool" factor as a result of his having played quarterback at a Big Twelve school, back in the day.

A few weeks after Lisa came on board, Chet announced an office reorganization. Desks, cubicles, and a few of the smaller offices were shuffled, amidst the usual grumpiness of those who felt, for whatever reason, disadvantaged by their new station. Hey, some gotta' win, and some gotta' lose. Right?

Lisa won. The Director of Development now had an office right next door to . . . guess who? Correct. Chet thought Lisa's relocation was an excellent way to send a message that development was a new priority for the school.

Of course Lisa's proximity to the Principal's office also made it inevitable that the two would have more opportunities to interact. This was fine, of course, at first. But at some point Lisa thought it strange that whenever she was headed for the kitchen for a cup of coffee, Chet showed up to suggest that they have a cup together. And it always seemed like Chet was around to greet her in the morning, and to wish her a good evening at the end of the day.

Before too long, Chet's interest in Lisa went beyond strange. Unwelcome sexual advances in a workplace environment are actionable. Lisa had had enough.

There are few other things that can take the wind out of the sails of a program to raise funds for a non-profit organization faster than a well-publicized sex scandal. Lisa's lawyers had a keen sense of their leverage. By notifying the school's counsel of Lisa's claims before filing suit, and by inviting a confidential, private mediation, Lisa's lawyers knew they were maximizing her opportunity to achieve a quick, and favorable, outcome.

The school's trustees and lawyers quickly accepted the invitation to mediate. Still, who was telling the truth?

Chet was denying everything. Happily married and the father of young children, Chet's position was that he was offended by the accusations. Chet had an explanation for everything. The office move. The invitation to Lisa to join him at a conference of private school administrators. In Las Vegas. The congratulations card to celebrate Lisa's three-month anniversary at the school (even though no one else had ever been the recipient of such recognition).

Lisa's lawyers also had a keen sense of the mediation process. Before the mediation, they met with me privately, and shared with me all of the facts that they assumed Chet had passed along to his lawyers. Along with one or two others. And they told me that I had discretion to reveal these other facts to Chet's lawyers at an appropriate time, if I thought it would be helpful.

Finally the big day arrived. Lisa was represented by very fine lawyers. Lawyers who represent clients like Lisa always have a conflict. Lisa's lawyers absolutely had an interest in producing a result consistent with Lisa's needs and desires. Lisa wanted to be compensated, of course, but she wanted Chet removed from the school. Lisa wanted vindication, of course, but she had no desire for her claims to become public, and publicized. Lisa was angry, of course, but she wanted resolution of this matter quickly, quietly, and efficiently.

Lisa's lawyers also had a multitude of interests. In addition to satisfying her interests, the lawyers wanted to earn as large a fee as possible, and these are the kinds of cases that wind up in the news media, generating attention, and possibly new cases, for the lawyers.

Chet was also well represented. Not only were lawyers present retained by the school to defend Chet and the interests of the school, Chet had wisely hired his own lawyer, and was paying the lawyer out of his own funds. But also present were lawyers and claims representatives for the school's "officers and directors" liability insurance carrier.

Yes, we had quite a crowd that day, all to deal with a classic "he said, she said" dispute.

The negotiations lasted all morning, and into the afternoon. Lisa's grossly excessive demands continued to draw ridiculous low-ball offers from the school and its insurer.

Then late in the afternoon, I decided it was time.

"Chet, tell me about the earrings." Lawyers on both sides of Chet, and at the end of the table, as a chorus in response to my inquiry, said, "What earrings?"

We were starting to make progress.

Lisa's lawyers had explained to me that for her birthday, after she had only been at the school for about four weeks, Chet had given her a pair of sapphire and diamond earrings. And, they speculated, this was a fact so incriminating that it was unlikely that Chet had had the courage to pass along this juicy tidbit to his lawyers.

The speculation was accurate.

Very distinctive beads of sweat began to roll down both sides of Chet's face, as the newly inquisitive eyes and minds of his legal team bore in on him. "Look, it's completely harmless. I happened to be at a mall when I suddenly remembered that the next day was her birthday. She had just started and was doing such an excellent job, and I was standing right next to a jewelry store . . . ."

"Chet," I replied when his sweat-soaked rambling finally concluded. "Wouldn't a plant have been more practical?"

I advised Chet and his legal team that I would step out and give them a chance to assess the situation. One can only imagine the inquisition Chet suffered behind that closed door. Poor Chet.

The case settled for a reasonable sum of money about three hours and Chet's resignation later.

One of the virtues of mediation, in some instances, is that it is off-the-record and confidential. In most jurisdictions all communication between the parties, counsel and the mediator may not be used again later for any purpose. To illustrate, if one party during the mediation acknowledges that she made a mistake, or even apologizes to the other side, it would not be permissible for opposing counsel, at a trial several months later, to ask that party on the witness stand, "Isn't it true that several months ago in the mediator's conference room, you acknowledged that you had caused the accident and you apologized to my client?"

No can do. This rule of mediation is intended, of course, to encourage candor and open communication.

The mediation of Lisa's claims against Chet provides an excellent example of how the confidentiality of the proceedings, and the right of one party to share anything with the mediator that the party might or might not want to be passed along to the other side, can be carefully used to produce resolution of a dispute quickly, quietly and efficiently.

Chet didn't get what he deserved. Chet was lucky.

CHAPTER 3

Choosing a Mediator

"Who is the best pitcher in baseball?" As of this writing the candidates appear to be Justin Verlander of the Detroit Tigers and Clayton Kershaw of the Los Angeles Dodgers. No doubt this will change by the time this book is in print. But to answer the question don't we need more information? Are we talking only about starting pitchers, or can we include closers? (Some of my friends are Yankees fans and for some reason they think Mariano Rivera is pretty good!) Can I know which team the pitcher will be facing and each pitcher's record against that particular team? Are we choosing a pitcher for Game 1 of the World Series, or Game 1 of a routine series in mid-June? Knowing more about the situation will inform our answer to the question, and may change our answer.

I am often asked, *"Who is the best mediator in town"*? My responses are always the same: "tell me about the dispute," and more importantly, "can you tell me about the people who will be participating in the mediation?"

All lawyers who regularly participate in mediations have their short list of favorite neutrals. Preferably, no lawyer has only one name on his list. There is a traditional set of qualifications sought in most cases: the mediator candidate should enjoy a solid reputation for integrity and honesty; the candidate should be someone who will disclose any circumstance that might affect his or her impartiality in the matter or that might create even the appearance of a conflict of interest. Any mediator you choose will be someone who has a proven track record as a neutral, or at least have enough legal, judicial, or practical experience to reassure each participant in the process of the neutral's credibility.

The Internet Is Your Friend

Websites are a good place to start when trying to find a mediator for your dispute. Whether a mediator is a "solo" (an independent lawyer or otherwise self-employed with no partners or associates), functions in a group of mediators sharing overhead, is in a law firm, or is on the roster of a neutral services provider, mediators tend to have websites that provide useful information.

The American Arbitration Association ("AAA") (www.adr.org) has been around forever, and is the flagship of the armada of dispute resolution service providers. AAA is an international, not-for profit organization, and its reach and resources are vast. Though usually thought of in connection with arbitration, the AAA website is also a comprehensive resource for mediation materials and information. AAA functions by maintaining rosters of neutrals, both arbitrators and mediators. Typically an AAA mediation is initiated by one of the parties to a contract that requires mediation and requires that AAA be used; the party contacts an AAA case manager. The case manager facilitates the process by learning a bit about the case, the parties and the lawyers, and then provides the parties with a list of mediator candidates, including a summary of their backgrounds and qualifications. AAA does not, ordinarily, publish bios for their roster members on the website, so you will not find out about the qualifications of your candidates until furnished with a pre-selected list by the case manager. Through a process of ranking certain candidates and disqualifying others, a mediator is finally selected. The case manager remains involved by assisting with the confirmation of date, place and time of the mediation, invoicing and collecting fees, and perhaps coordinating the pre-mediation submissions of the parties. Note that the typical AAA mediation does not begin by one side contacting a mediator who happens to be on an AAA roster. AAA mediations are managed by AAA, and fees are charged accordingly. Though AAA is a "non-profit," occasionally the parties will be unpleasantly surprised when the case management fees that are charged, on top of the mediator's fee, seem unnecessary or excessive. On the other hand, the case manager may provide valuable services throughout the process.

Judicial Arbitration & Mediation Services ("JAMS") (www.jamsadr.com) is a national, for-profit service provider. JAMS was the creation of visionary founders in California in the 1980's. The original JAMS model was to create rosters of neutrals in various markets made up entirely of former judges (thus the name). As JAMS expanded nationally, the model was more successful in some markets than others, depending on the local availability of former members of the judiciary. But overall JAMS has been highly successful and is highly regarded, even though some markets now include neutrals on the JAMS roster without judicial experience. JAMS publishes bios of its neutrals on its website, and uses case managers and charges case management fees. A JAMS mediation can begin by one side's contacting JAMS, but can also begin when a side contacts her favorite neutral, who happens to be with JAMS. JAMS has successfully marketed its services over the years by persuading institutional litigants such as banks and insurance companies to write "JAMS" into mediation and arbitration clauses in all sorts of contracts. Rumor has it that JAMS can be a bit pricey; I'm sure my friends at JAMS would argue that you get what you pay for!

It is a mouthful to say "International Center for Conflict Prevention & Resolution," so happily this group is better known by its acronym, CPR (www.cpr.org). CPR is a national and international organization that promotes and facilitates ADR in a variety of ways. CPR maintains rosters of neutrals (to be on the roster, and I am on their roster, you pay an annual fee), publishes a variety of rules for mediation and arbitration, and hosts conferences and training programs. It is similar to AAA in several respects, though not nearly as widely known or used. In certain respects it appears that CPR is trying to achieve a special niche in the ADR field by providing what it refers to as a "non-administered" process. By non-administered, CPR means that when a case is submitted, a case manager may assist the parties with the selection of the neutral, but then the case manager gracefully exits the scene, leaving it to the neutral to take over scheduling, billing, convening, etc. The goal is to save the participants the expense of case management. CPR should be an extremely attractive option for disputing parties who want *some* structure (rules, initial direction, and so forth), but not *a lot* of structure.

A number of other ADR organizations focus on being a resource for mediators and arbitrators, while remaining a resource for disputing parties in search of an experienced neutral. On this list you will find the National Academy of Distinguished Neutrals ("NADN") (www.nadn.org), the Association of Attorney-Mediators ("AAM") (www.attorney-mediators.org), and Mediate.com (www.mediate.com). I am proud to be a member of NADN and find it to be different than most of the other organizations in a couple of respects. First, NADN rosters are "invitation only" (you can't just sign up by paying an annual fee, so the quality of the rosters in the markets where NADN operates is consistently high). Second, most of the members maintain their calendars on a common website. So if you know a location, a date, and the type of dispute that needs to be mediated, you can go to a single website, do a simple search, and find a list of experienced and qualified mediators available on your desired date.

Word of Mouth

Popular magazines on newsstands, popularity polls taken by local bar associations, and individual mediator advertising on the internet can also be consulted during a mediator search.

But the best method for finding the right mediator is usually to consult with lawyers or others who have experience participating in mediations, people you know who can reliably comment on the strengths and weaknesses of various mediator candidates.

Sometimes I learn that I was on a list of potential mediators in a case, but someone else was ultimately chosen. This used to hurt my feelings, until I figured out that I may not have been the best choice! Perhaps the participants felt they needed someone younger. Or older. Or someone with more judicial experience. Or someone with a degree in electrical engineering. Or someone neither side had ever used as a mediator before. Or a non-lawyer.

Mediators have a range of skills and experience, each mediator has his or her own personality, and each case will have special circumstances that may need consideration when selecting a neutral. But are there factors that we can say should be applied generically, across-the-board, when trying to find the right neutral for a particular matter?

Substance Expertise

There are disputes where "substance expertise" is essential. A case alleging that source code for software has been misappropriated may benefit from a neutral who has a computer science background and the technical training that allows him or her to speak the technical language and understand the issues that will be on the table in the mediation. When a dispute is all about accounting issues, a mediator with an accounting background may be uniquely helpful.

A subset of substance expertise is *legal expertise*: when someone asks, "Do you have experience in banking regulation?", my answer is "no," and then I try to provide a recommendation as to others the caller may want to contact. A dispute over an ERISA benefit plan may benefit from using a mediator with legal knowledge of the statutory framework in which ERISA exists.

Family Law Is Different

Family law matters (divorce and child custody cases) are one area where non-lawyer mediators have thrived and are well accepted. This has to do, in part, with the issues traditionally in dispute in these cases: tracing and the characterization of an asset as "community" or "personal" property; the valuation of an ongoing business or some other asset; the factors regarding the best interests of the children of the marriage; and mental health issues. While knowledge of the local court system and the predelictions of the judge before whom the case is pending may be of interest, the non-lawyer mediator may have sufficient experience and other skills that outweigh the value assigned to having legal training.

Process Expertise

But outside isolated cases where narrow, technical issues are paramount, or esoteric legal issues are on the table, or in the marital discord context, the cases that need a neutral with "substance expertise" are relatively few. More often what is needed is a neutral with "process expertise," someone with experience and demonstrated ability in dispute resolution. In other words, *substance expertise* is necessary *sometimes*, but *process expertise* is necessary *every time*. Most experienced mediators probably view themselves as experts in the *process* of facilitating communication and resolution.

If you can find both substance and process expertise in the same individual (and they are out there) expect to pay handsomely for their services!

Evaluative vs. Non-Evaluative

There are as many styles of mediating as there are mediators, but when required to attempt to categorize them, many commentators suggest that there are, essentially, two styles, two schools of thought as to the proper role and function of the mediator. Knowing who will be participating in your upcoming mediation, you may want to consider which general approach you think will work best.

Many believe that mediators should be "non-evaluative". Regardless of whether they have an opinion about which side is "right" and which side is "wrong", such an opinion should never be expressed. From this perspective, mediators should be facilitative and not directive and the expression of an opinion or evaluation means that the neutral is no longer "neutral".

In the other camp are those who strongly believe that mediators should be evaluative and not be reluctant to share their opinions. This is why some former judges are highly sought after mediators. Former judges are accustomed to forming opinions, and expressing them, and their service on the bench can lend a substantial amount of credibility to their evaluation of a case. But I have long had a general view of mediators with judicial experience on their resume: the longer their service on the bench, the less effective they are likely to be as mediators. Years of service on the bench may mean that the former jurist grew accustomed to directing outcomes, and to expecting others to follow her orders. These will very rarely be useful traits in a mediator.

I am a champion of evaluative mediation. I have opinions. I express them. My experience, credibility, and reputation, as well as my ability to evaluate cases, is why people come to see me. Mediators should not, in my view, argue with one side that their case is terrible and their prospects poor, and then argue the opposite view with their adversary. Effective mediators have integrity. Whatever are the views of the evaluative mediator, they should not change from room to room.

I believe that the evaluative mediation model is the more popular model for a reason. I once had a general counsel for a Fortune 500 company as a guest in an ADR class I was teaching, and she told the class, "If I hear Professor Pryor use the word 'neutral' one more time, I'm going to throw up. At my company when we mediate we don't want 'neutral.' We want a mediator who has opinions and will express them".

Neutrality

This word gets thrown about a lot in the discussion of mediators and mediation. Mediators are supposed to be neutral, and to communicate their neutrality in word and deed. Mediation training devotes a great deal of its attention to role playing exercises in which the neutrality of the trainee is scrutinized, criticized, and rehearsed again and again. The demonstrated ability to maintain neutrality should definitely be a consideration in the selection process.

In the joint session, during the presentation by Party A, did the mediator put her pen down, turn her chair to face the presenter, and hold her head a bit to one side in rapt attention? Then, during the presentation by Party B, it is imperative that the mediator put her pen down, turn her chair to face the presenter, and hold her head a bit to one side in rapt attention! If the mediator takes notes during one presentation, she must take notes during the other. Believe me, it matters.

Spoken language matters, as well. A mediator doesn't describe a party's claim as "frivolous"; it is "challenging" or "extremely creative." The point a party just made with great emphasis is not "irrelevant"; instead, it is "not as relevant as other points." The lawyer is not "arrogant"; the lawyer is "very self- confident"!

Years ago I conducted a joint session in a medical malpractice case and thought, quite naturally, that I did a fabulous job! But the plaintiff's lawyer, one of the finest medical malpractice lawyers in the state and someone I greatly respected, grabbed me in the hallway after I split the parties up and said, "Will, my client is FURIOUS with you; you have really created a problem." I was horrified, as well as mystified, and it showed. "Will, do you realize that every time you referred to my client (the Plaintiff) in the joint session you referred to him by his first name, and every time you referred to the Defendant, you referred to him as 'Dr. ___'? My client feels totally disrespected".

As I was saying, neutral language is important.

But the ability of the mediator to conduct the process in an even, neutral fashion is not first tested in the joint session at the mediation. The neutral's ability to both *be neutral* and *be perceived as neutral* begins with the very first contact received from a lawyer, secretary, paralegal, claims representative or other participant.

To illustrate: I was contacted by email by a paralegal for one of the attorneys who had inquired about my available dates because, I was told, both sides had agreed to use me as a mediator. In my email response to the paralegal, I used her first name, as in "Thanks, Lisa, for your inquiry; here are my available dates"; I also included "Thanks, Lisa, *as always*, for your inquiry; here are my available dates." I later learned that it was the "as always" expression that caused the other side to determine that I was too familiar with their opposing counsel, and so they disqualified me.

When the participants to the mediation arrive at my office in the morning, and the receptionist gets the parties situated in their assigned conference rooms while I make the rounds and introduce myself and make certain that we have everyone expected to attend, I have learned the hard way that it is important that I not be seen by Party A emerging from the conference room assigned to Party B. To do so can create an uneasiness that the mediator is not neutral, but instead is giving one side attention before both sides receive attention. Silly? Absolutely! Important? You bet!

A final thought about neutrality. Too often when a participant hears that the person sitting at the end of the table claims to be "neutral," the conclusion is drawn that "neutral" means "indifferent," and I think it is important that the participants understand the distinction. Though I am neutral throughout the mediation process, I am not indifferent as to whether the process is helpful to both sides. I may not care what the terms of the settlement agreement turn out to be, but it matters to me whether a settlement is achieved. I care about whether the process is successful, and I want the participants to know it.

It's a Money Thing: Fees

The fees charged by the mediator are varied, and depend on a range of factors: the local market for neutral services; the availability of experienced neutrals; the size and complexity of the dispute (perhaps); the number of parties participating in the fee; and the fee structure of the individual mediator.

In very modest cases (modest does not mean unimportant, modest means small dollar), many court systems rely on mediators willing to donate their services for no charge (to hone their skills and to improve their marketing claims as to their experience), and there may be local dispute resolution clinics sponsored by the local courts, local governments, law schools, or bar associations, where mediators are available for a modest charge, perhaps $50 per party for a two-hour mediation, or for no charge. So exploring the availability of these low-cost options is a worthwhile exercise in many cases. The mediator might not have a vast amount of experience, and the mediation might occur in a vacant courtroom, jury room, or some other relatively unpretentious environment, but the process itself and the opportunity for a neutral facilitator to assist two sides to a dispute should be no different in many respects than the mediation of a dispute arising from an oil spill in the Gulf of Mexico.

On the other end of the spectrum are the mediations of large commercial and insurance disputes, some lasting days, in which experienced neutrals (the ones with substance AND process expertise) are expected to spend several days in pre-mediation conferences and in studying briefs and other materials.   Fees for this type of mediation can reach into six figures.

But in most cases, in most markets, an experienced mediator's fee will usually run from several hundred dollars per party, to perhaps a few thousand dollars, for a full-day mediation. Some cases are scheduled on a "half day" basis, and the mediator's fee is reduced accordingly. There are still mediators in many markets who, like a lot of lawyers, will charge an hourly rate. I have never thought this was good idea. In my experience the mediation process is inevitably boring and tedious for some of the participants, and almost always takes longer to reach resolution or impasse than the parties thought was necessary. I never want to create a reason, and an hourly rate would be a reason, for any participant in one of my mediations to think that the process seems to be taking forever because I am trying to drag it out to generate a bigger fee. Most mediators are "flat rate" service providers, and my overall experience is that most parties like the fact that they need not worry about being surprised by a second or third invoice following the mediation.

Do you get what you pay for? Many years ago I was mediating an insurance coverage dispute between a municipality that had experienced some damage to its water and sewer system due to a violent storm, and an insurance company that insured some, but not all, of the repairs the municipality claimed were necessary. The city brought a fleet of representatives: the City Attorney, a couple of City Council members, city risk managers, water and sewer construction people and outside litigation and coverage counsel. The insurance company, of course, was similarly well represented. For several hours we made no progress. The lead outside counsel for the insurance company was a superb lawyer, a perfect gentleman, a senior name partner at one of the city's finest firms, a man who embodied professionalism and old-school civility (he never removed his suit coat throughout the day; in fact, he never unbuttoned it). This gentleman exuded class. But the reason we weren't making any progress was because he believed that the City's opening demand was exactly twice what it should be. The formula the City was using to calculate its damages was flawed, he said, and he wouldn't allow his insurance company client to make an offer until the demand was cut in half. In the politest way imaginable, we were getting absolutely nowhere, as back and forth I shuttled between the parties. Lunch arrived. Still no movement. But around 2:00 in the afternoon the city representatives had a "light bulb" moment, and realized he was right. "Will", the City said, "tell the insurance company we are terribly sorry it took us so long to figure this out, but he is correct, and we are willing to cut our demand in half."

With great joy I entered the insurance company's conference room and reported this exciting development. My friend the esteemed, wise counsel, paused, looked all around the table of representatives he had assembled for the occasion, and said very slowly, "That's wonderful. Now we can go use one of those mediators who doesn't charge so much."

Yes, mediators hear everything about the fees they charge!

I would like to think that there is usually a direct correlation between the amount of the fee charged and the quality of the service provided by a neutral mediator. The free market has a way of sorting these things out. Like attorneys whose hourly rates can vary from some to a lot, mediators tend to charge what the market will bear. If they are popular, they will raise their rates. If things are slow, they may reduce their rates.

Regardless of the total amount of the fee, the custom and practice in most markets, in most agreements to mediate, and in court mediation orders is for the total fee to be divided evenly between the parties. Occasionally, there will be a circumstance when one party agrees to pay the entire fee (perhaps one side asked the Court for a continuance and suggested mediation, and the other side protested and pointed out that the case had already been mediated, so the party seeking the relief offered to pay the whole fee), but the "best practice" and most common practice is for the fee to be divided. And every mediator I know is appreciative when the parties are careful to make payment of the fee prior to the convening of the mediation.

Let's Not Get Too Cozy

When the matter being mediated is a pending lawsuit, there is often a perception by the participants that the mediator is something of an adjunct of the court. This is partially true, and the mediator's relationship with the court in which the matter is pending should not be overlooked.

Most mediation referral schemes in most states include an obligation that the mediator report to the court on the outcome of the process. Under its preferred version, this obligation is limited to advising the court that the matter was successfully resolved, that it reached an impasse, or that the mediator will be continuing to work with the parties. There is an ongoing debate in the ADR community about whether it is appropriate to consider going beyond the "thumbs up" or "thumbs down" reporting scheme, that maybe we should be authorizing mediators to advise the court of the positions of the parties, or at least some next steps that the court might want to consider to encourage resolution. What could be wrong, goes the argument, with letting the court know that one of the hindrances to settlement was that one party is still hopeful that its motion to dismiss the case will be granted by the court, if the court will ever get around to ruling on it! Or perhaps it wouldn't violate a confidence if the mediator revealed to the court that the parties reached a stalemate because the court has declined to set the case for trial for over a year, and one party views delay as their friend!

In theory the rule could require mediators to report on actual substance, opining on which party was reasonable in the mediation and which party unreasonable. Why not, goes the argument, since we have long experienced the settlement conference with the judge, in which the judge brings subtle and not-so-subtle pressure to bear on parties to settle.

Whenever these kinds of arguments are advanced, the ADR community rolls out a plethora of "thin end of the wedge," "slippery slope," and "camel's nose under the tent" protests. Most neutrals view the concept of more mediator communication with the court as so highly problematic, so fraught with risk, we just don't want to even begin going down that path. *If it ain't broke, don't fix it.* Or if it's a little bit broke, the attempted repair is likely to make the situation worse. Kind of like repairs I attempt around my house!

I have had the experience of receiving a telephone call from a federal judge on a Friday afternoon during the mediation of a case headed for a two-week jury trial in that judge's court the following Monday morning. "How's it going?", asked the judge. The judge was desperately eager for information. I was lucky. The judge calling me understood the proper parameters of the conversation, and knew that it would be inappropriate to directly ask me to provide any information. "I hope to have good news in a couple of hours, Your Honor," was all I said. "Good," she replied. "We'll be down here waiting for your call." Talk about pressure!

But it is easy to imagine that some judges will not be so sensitive to the proper scope of such a conversation, and in one form or fashion will inevitably try to squeeze information out of the mediator.

From time to time one party or the other will encourage the mediator to disclose more than is proper.

All of this is why the mediator's reputation for integrity, and the mediator's relationship with the court, may be worth consideration.

What a Mediator Should NOT Do

Physicians are supposed to be mindful of the "first, do no harm" rule. Perhaps mediators should be mindful as well.

As a mediator you will inevitably encounter parties who are emotionally vulnerable. There will be parties in your mediations who have lost a loved one, or their career or business, or a dream. You will deal with parties who are grieving. And you will confront a conflict between doing everything that you are trained to do and know how to do to achieve a settlement, and the need that the vulnerable party may have to go forward with his or her dispute. Your mediation may not be the right time, or the right place, for them to let go.

In a mediation in which issues of emotional well-being may be tested, consider using a professional neutral with the training and background to properly handle it.

I Choose Your Guy

A final note on choosing a mediator. If you reach the point where you and your opponent are proposing candidates to serve as your neutral, try, whenever possible and within reason, to agree to a candidate recommended by your opponent. In doing so you will create a positive dynamic at the mediation. Your adversary will not be able to complain about the process, the mediator, or the mediator's evaluation. Your adversary is invested in the choice of the mediator. You, on the other hand, can complain away!

Time to Choose: Let's Pick a Mediator!

Mediator A is two years out of law school, has yet to try a case to a jury, has never handled an employment case, but has excellent skills and instincts as a mediator, and offers this at the mediation: "Mr. Plaintiff, I listened to you describe what happened to you, and while I'm very sympathetic, I must tell you that the most likely outcome in your case if you take it to trial is that you will lose. In fact, if you tried your case to ten different juries, I wouldn't expect you to prevail more than once."

Mediator B was on the local trial bench for fifteen years, presiding over 900 jury trials, after ten years in private practice specializing in employment law, and offers this at the mediation, "Mr. Plaintiff, thank you for sharing with me the details of how your employer mistreated you. It must have been quite a challenge to deal with it. But as the former judge for fifteen years of the court in which your case is pending, I'm afraid I've got some bad news for you—your case is too hard to pursue. The most likely scenarios going forward if you walk out of here today are that you will receive nothing for your claim".

There is no comparison between the credibility of Mediator A and Mediator B. Mediator A may have a great future in the field of dispute resolution, may be smart, and may have done really well in law school. But there are reasons why Mediator B, *all other considerations being equal*, is likely to be more effective as the mediator of the dispute.

But what do we mean by "all other considerations being equal"? Mediator A may still be the best choice! Is it not possible that Mediator A, because of age, gender, race, ethnicity, or sheer personality, might be someone the plaintiff is more likely to trust, and listen to? Does Mediator B have a condition lawyers sometimes call "judge-itis": after a few years on the bench and having lawyers bow to them every day, they become arrogant, condescending and insufferable? Does Mediator A demonstrate patience, a sense of humor, empathy, and obvious preparation for the mediation? Does Mediator B, while having superior credentials, appear uninterested in anything other than getting paid and having the parties figure out that what they need to do is follow his directives, like they have been doing every day for the past 15 years, and by the way, it's a beautiful afternoon and we don't want anything to interfere with that 2:30 tee time, do we?

Qualifications matter, but other considerations matter as well.

At the End of the Day

John was thrilled when Kyle, a buddy from a baseball camp he had attended, invited him to come for a week-long visit to Kyle's family farm a couple of hundred miles from the city where John lived. Parents conferred with parents to make certain there were no reservations, and the teenagers were allowed to hang out together on the farm.

John was a city boy, and he had never ridden a tractor, or any other piece of farm equipment. When Kyle said, "Come on, I'll show you how," John eagerly jumped into the driver's seat. Within moments he lost control. The tractor hit a stump and knocked John off his seat and under the giant rear wheel of the machine. John's neck was crushed, and he died instantly.

John was an only child, the pride and joy of his parents, a bright, enthusiastic, popular and friendly boy, and an excellent baseball prospect, as well.

At the mediation of the lawsuit filed against Kyle's parents, alleging negligent supervision, John's parents were still in shock over the tragedy. As with anyone going through the stages of grief, theirs was an excrutiating journey, and they had a long way to go. Fortunately, they had an extremely fine lawyer who cared about them, and was sensitive to the possibility that it was too soon to be trying to resolve the case. But they said they wanted to put it all behind them, and for various other reasons, lawyer and clients felt it was the right time. So here they were in my conference room.

This was one of those cases when a joint session was deemed a potential hazard, and so all participants, including the insurance carriers representing the defendant couple, agreed to dispense with it.

John's parents made an opening demand. The opening demand was for the insurance policy limits ($500,000.00), an amount that they would require be matched by personal funds of Kyle's family. The total amount would be stipulated to be a gift to the local high school, to build a new baseball facility for the school that would be named to honor John's memory. The messages in the opening demand were clear: "We have experienced pain and we are not going to settle until you experience pain as well—this case will not be settled only with insurance company money"; and "we don't want or need the money, the money is not for us, the money is so that others will remember our boy."

The initial private caucus with Kyle's parents, the lawyers and the insurers began. Kyle's parents, unsurprisingly, were in a deep psychological hole. Their guilt seemed to be matched only by their inability to meaningfully contribute their own money to the settlement; any substantial amount of money from them would require them to sell the family farm. They felt horrible, but also felt that this is why they had secured liability insurance. They absolutely wanted this nightmare to go away—with insurance money.

The insurers were hard to budge. This was just an accident. This was just teenage boys doing what teenage boys do. This was a horrible accident, a tragedy, but it did not mean that their insureds were liable for anything. But they would be willing to make an offer, given the uncertainty, the cost of defense, and so forth.

What the insurers then proposed stunned me. They had brought along with them a "structured settlement specialist." Structured settlements are common in cases in which a minor child is going to receive a decent amount of money, or a lot of money, for his or her injury or for the loss of a parent. A structured settlement usually involves the purchase of annuities with the settlement proceeds. In most states, the "structured" aspect of the settlement has to be approved by the court, but then is a locked-in benefit for the child once the child turns 18. Structured settlements can be wonderful. They can provide a significant tax advantage to the beneficiary, and the annuity can be set up to fund a college education, to provide a monthly income, to provide a substantial payment at ages 21, 25, 30, etc., or, if there is enough money involved, all of the above. There is nothing wrong, per se, with structured settlements.

The negotiation of a structured settlement ordinarily will take place on the back end of a negotiation, not with the very first offer made. To illustrate, if the negotiation of a claim involving the injury to a child has come down to a gap of $750,000 vs. $600,000, in order to close the gap an insurance company may begin illustrating how the funds could be structured. Perhaps $250,000 will be shown to be cash up front, to deal with medical bills, immediate medical needs of the child, and attorney's fees. The balance of $350,000 is plugged into a computer program, and an "illustration" is printed out, illustrating how in 30 years the $350,000 will actually have paid out an exponentially greater total. *Illustrations are both a legitimate tool, and a negotiation tool. Insurers are always hopeful that unsophisticated claimants will see the "total" in the illustration and be swept off their feet.*

It is this aspect of the "illustration" that will sometimes create tension in a negotiation. It is an issue that sometimes requires a diplomatic touch. I have had plaintiff's lawyers say, "Will, tell the insurance company down the hall that if they send you in here one more time with an illustration we are leaving." Why is offense taken? Because to some plaintiff's counsel, the use of the illustration implies a message that the lawyer is either too dumb and unsophisticated to appreciate the benefits of a structure (the reality is that most plaintiff's lawyers in substantial cases have had their own annuity brokers working on the case several days prior to the mediation), or worse, the lawyer is unethical and hasn't explained to the client that money properly invested can have long-term benefits (insurers sometimes assume that all plaintiffs lawyers only want all the money up front, and so they don't counsel their client's appropriately). The tension is greatest when the insurer instructs the mediator, "when you take this illustration into the plaintiff's room, make sure you personally hand it to the parents and not the lawyer, and make sure they see the number at the bottom of the page."

Believe me, when it gets this heavy-handed, offense can be taken.

What was wrong with the insurers for Kyle's parents handing me illustrations to support their initial offer? Everything.

First, John's parents were substantial people who didn't need anyone to explain to them the wisdom of investing money.

Second, John's parents had just explained that they didn't want money, they wanted to do something to honor John's memory; it's hard to build a high school baseball facility with an annuity.

Third, there wasn't a minor child receiving the benefits of the settlement, so protecting and saving the money made little sense.

Fourth, the illustrations ignored the requirement laid down in the initial demand that Kyle's parents experience some of the "pain."

Fifth, the structure was being advanced at the very outset of the negotiation, not as a bridge at the end to close the deal.

Finally, given the fragile emotional state of John's parents and where we were in the negotiation, I thought that what the insurers wanted to do was the demonstration of almost cruel insensitivity to the circumstances.

At first I tried my best to be polite: "You know, I love to discuss structures and it's great that we may be able to use a structure as a component in getting this matter resolved, but let's just save the discussion for later on and stick with the basics for right now."

Insurers: "No, Will, we think it would be best for you to show them what this money could turn into. We think they will be impressed."

Me: "I just have to disagree. It's a timing thing. I think we would be better off acknowledging their interest in doing something for the baseball program at his school, and see where it goes."

Insurers: "Will, we do this all the time and you would be amazed at how effective this can be. We want you to go in there and try to sell it."

This dialogue went on for awhile. I was stalling for time, doing everything I could to talk them out of making the initial offer in the manner they were insisting upon. I wanted them to just take the money they were proposing to structure, and offer it as cash. It would at least buy a new batting cage! Nothing worked. Finally, I did something that I don't think I had ever done in a mediation before, or have done since. I begged.

Me: "Look. If you make me do this I have to do it. But I have been in the room with these folks and I think that what you are proposing is a horrible idea. I am begging you to not make me do it."

The insurers were unrelenting. At some point a mediator has to remind himself that he is, after all, just the mediator!

I trudged down the hall, illustrations in hand, vowing to do the best I could.

I sat down at the conference table across from John's parents. I asked them how they were doing, whether they were comfortable with what was happening, just trying to engage them in pleasant conversation. Then as casually and nonchalantly as possible, I nudged the illustrations across the table in their direction, and said "These aren't anything to take too seriously at this point, but the insurers asked me to share them with you. I know your lawyer has counseled you on how this process works, that where we start out usually doesn't have anything to do with where we might end up. Blah. Blah. Blah." In other words, I was filibustering. By blathering on I was hoping to de-fuse the situation.

But I trailed off when I noticed that the mom was beginning to tremble. And then she stood up and began trembling a lot. Her husband stood up next to her. She was enraged. She leaned across the table towards me and screamed: "If you (pointing at me) think my son's life is worth the amount on this piece of paper then f___ you and f___ this whole thing!" She wadded up the paper, threw it, and it hit me in the face.

The couple stormed out of the conference room, slamming the door as hard as it could be slammed, never to return. The mediation was over.

The purpose for telling this story is to illustrate how complicated the mediation task can become when some in the mix are emotionally vulnerable. In the process of selecting a neutral, should not more consideration have been given to the emotional state of these people? Setting aside that mediating the case was premature, and that the qualifications of the mediator were likely irrelevant, why not involve a mental health specialist in the mediation? Why not use a professional counselor in place of a process expert, or to supplement the process expert? Once I was in the saddle and the mediation was underway, I felt horribly inadequate to the task of helping these people. They so obviously didn't need a mediator on that day; they needed a therapist, and a pastor. Mediators should be mindful that, at the end of the day, most of us are not therapists, healers, or counselors. Most of us are just lawyers with dispute resolution skills.

CHAPTER 4

Preparing for the Mediation

Preparing for a mediation is simple. It merely requires a bit of thought, and a bit of anticipation. Who will be present? What has caused this dispute to require a mediation to resolve it? Is the challenge opposing counsel? Is the obstacle a client on the other side with an attitude, or at least unrealistic expectations? How will you best use the mediation to your advantage? What is your *plan*?

Negotiation is not just about persuasion; it's also about creating doubt. In preparing for your next mediation, anticipate the opportunity and think about the dynamics that you want to create. *By what means do you intend to create doubt in the mind of your adversary?* If you are an attorney, do you intend to rely on *your* skills as an advocate, or *your client's* ability to communicate his or her position? Should there be a joint session—an opportunity to communicate directly with the other side—or should you discuss with the mediator the possibility that a joint session will be counterproductive?

Another way of looking at your goal in preparing for mediation is to ask, "what can I provide the mediator that will help the mediator understand my case, and turn the mediator into an advocate for my position when meeting with the other party?" This is the fundamental challenge of the process; the neutral will remain neutral, but giving the well-prepared mediator tools to assist you is how you seize the advantage.

So preparation means not only preparing yourself, but preparing a client and certainly preparing the mediator.

Participation Matters: Who Will Attend?

Consideration of who should be and will be physically present at and participating in the mediation is another fundamental item on your preparation checklist. In a dispute where Fred is making a claim against Joe, Fred and Joe need to be present. But in other circumstances, it may not be as straightforward and the issue deserves attention.

The issue of personal participation in mediation is too often overlooked. In most jurisdictions, a court order to mediate will include an order that all named parties attend, as well as representatives of an entity with "full authority" to agree to a settlement. This is as it should be. Any experienced mediator will tell you that when one side or the other is allowed to participate by phone, or when a corporate representative must make phone calls all day long to get directions and authorization as to how to proceed, the likelihood of success of the process plummets. After conducting over 3,000 mediations, I believe this this point is not an opinion, it is a fact. *The success of the process depends on the physical presence and participation of decision makers.* Memorize that last sentence! It is true regardless of how well-intentioned the parties are in agreeing to "phone" participation. If the parties are seriously committed to trying to resolve a dispute, they will be present. If they are not present, they are not committed. "My client promises that he will be glued to the phone and available every second." "The money saved from travel costs for my client to be here will help settle the case." My rear end! Don't believe it! I have dozens of examples of impasses that would not have happened if the person we were supposed to be able to reach at any time we needed to got on the line. I have dozens more examples of impasses that occurred when we were able to get the person we needed on the line, but it was apparent he was completely distracted or unable to get his thought process lined up and tuned in with what the rest of us had been working on for hours.

Want to suck the energy out of a negotiation? See what happens at a critical moment in the process when it completely shuts down for around two hours because someone is out to lunch, walking their dog, in an important meeting, forgot to turn the ringer to their cell phone on, etc. *Participation matters every time.*

Anyone experienced with the process also knows the feeling of showing up at the mediator's office, and noticing in the reception area that the other side's representative is the "wrong" person. Oh dear. "The other side is represented by the same adjuster whose poor judgment two years ago in denying our claim is what this dispute is all about!" "The other side has brought the same department head whose harassment and retaliation against my client is the basis for our claim!" In other words, the other side brought someone to make the decision to settle or not settle *whose fingerprints are on the murder weapon!* The process has not even begun and you and your client know the process is doomed, and your time and money that day wasted.

You, as an advocate for your client, have the ability to prevent this from happening.

As suggested above, most jurisdictions have a statute, a regulation, or a set of court rules that address the participation issue. In my state, the rule for decades has been this:

Authority of representatives. PARTY REPRESENTATIVES MUST HAVE AUTHORITY TO SETTLE AND ALL PERSONS NECESSARY TO THE DECISION TO SETTLE SHALL BE PRESENT.

Almost every lawyer in town is familiar with this requirement. But despite decades of mediation "everywhere, all the time," almost no one seems to be aware of the next part of the rule:

THE NAMES AND ADDRESSES OF SUCH PERSONS SHALL BE COMMUNICATED IN WRITING TO ALL PARTIES AND TO THE MEDIATOR.

While advocates, judges and commentators disagree over the meaning of "authority to settle" or "necessary to the decision to settle," or what the expressions *should* mean, what is clear is that as a participant in an upcoming mediation, you are entitled to know, *prior* to the event, who the other side intends to bring to the table. Even if you live in a jurisdiction that does not have such a rule, it would be surprising indeed if any mediator in a court-appointed mediation, if alerted prior to the mediation of a concern about participation, would not comply with a request to direct the parties to exchange the names of the participants who will be in attendance. This prior disclosure won't solve the problem every time, but it will solve the problem most of the time, and will at least save you the angst of discovering the problem in the mediator's reception area on the morning of the big event.

If the mediation is not court-ordered, but taking place by agreement, and on your side there is any level of concern about the other side's participation, then why aren't assurances about that participation *part of your agreement*?

I'm Talking About You

Now that we have reassured ourselves of the other side's commitment to the process, and maximized our chances of success, it would be wise to give consideration to the participation *on your side of the table*. This is the mirror image of the issue just discussed. You want a representative on your side who can be objective, and here's why.

Let's say your client's objective evaluation of the case is that it is willing to pay the other side $1.00. One dollar. That's o-n-e U.S. dollar. But your client representative has the "fingerprints" problem discussed previously; in other words, your client representative, in the eyes of your adversary, is the wrong person to be making decisions regarding settlement. All day long the mediator will have to deal with the other side's accusation that the only reason your client's position is unreasonable is *because* you have a biased decision maker. Bring the "wrong" person as a resource, but also bring his or her supervisor—almost anyone in the company higher up in the food chain will do. By doing so you eliminate or at least minimize the rant coming from down the hall about your side's objectivity. Your client's evaluation, and your offer, can still be one dollar, but you have created the appearance that you are at least *trying* to be objective.

An added bonus of ensuring that you had a fresh set of eyes in the mediation? Should the case not settle at mediation, and ultimately conclude weeks or months later at the courthouse in a manner not satisfactory to the client, you may have shielded yourself, a bit, from client concerns (and law partner concerns), that the mediation and settlement opportunities should have been handled differently.

Preparing the Mediator

We have a fine mediator, we are assured that all the key decision makers will be present, and the mediator has sent everyone a confirmation of the date, place and time of the mediation. Now what?

The next step is to communicate with the mediator. There are some mediators who will have an information form or case evaluation form for each side to fill out and submit in advance (I don't and never have—most people don't like filling out forms!). But typically the party or counsel on each side will submit at least a letter or memo summarizing the dispute, the procedural posture of the case, information about the court (if any) and trial setting, and perhaps a summary of any prior settlement negotiations. Usually included with such a letter are copies of key documents, perhaps copies of previous settlement demands or offers, and, if the dispute has become a pending lawsuit, copies of pleadings filed with the court. If the issues to be discussed at mediation include legal arguments, then copies of briefs and pertinent appellate court decisions may be included. This type of background information is fairly straightforward. In most jurisdictions there is no requirement to provide copies of anything submitted to the mediator to the other side; in other words, the written communication can be confidential, and the mediator can be instructed not to divulge anything contained in the submission without first obtaining permission to do so.

The fact that this sort of confidential communication with the mediator is not just allowed, but encouraged, is not of minor significance. A better practice than just a written submission is to take fuller advantage of the confidentiality cloak, and to call the mediator or schedule a telephone conference. In such a conversation, either the day before or perhaps a week prior to the mediation, you and the mediator can discuss any aspect of the case, and perhaps share topics best not put in writing. Does your client have a difficult personality, or inflated expectations? Tell the mediator. Do you and opposing counsel not get along? Give the mediator a heads up. Is it possible that the key to getting the matter resolved may be creating an opportunity for the clients to visit one-on-one, without the presence of counsel, but opposing counsel may resist? Let the mediator know, so that he or she can be looking for the right moment to make such a meeting the mediator's suggestion or request.

It is often the case that previous settlement negotiations are best discussed in a call, and not in writing. A negotiation dance, like a budding romance, can begin with very subtle overtures. A twenty or thirty minute conversation, unlike a written submission, is not a communication of just what you think the mediator *should* know, it includes those issues that the mediator *wants* to know.

But why stop here? If a phone call would be helpful, would not a meeting with the mediator be even better? Why not schedule a one-hour meeting at the mediator's office a few days before the mediation? Perhaps bring the client. Why not ask the mediator to come to your office for a meeting, or buy them lunch! And while we are on a roll, why not invite the mediator to meet with you and your client, *at your client's office*?

In my experience, these pre-mediation meetings are almost always helpful, and occasionally turn out to be critically important to the process of resolution. In a relaxed, unstructured environment, a few days before the mediation, without the pressure of other mediation participants waiting anxiously down the hall in another conference room, you may have a candid session with the mediator in which anything and everything can be discussed. When the big day comes, not only will the investment of this meeting time actually save the time of all participants at the mediation, but you have also allowed your experienced mediator an opportunity to anticipate the process and plan, to offer suggestions in your case about how the joint session should be conducted or whether there should even be a joint session, when and where the mediation should take place, what arguments to make at the beginning and which ones to save for the end, and where an appropriate and helpful starting point in the process of trading offers and demands might lie.

Not many cases will present an opportunity for a dramatic accident scene investigation (see essay at the end of this chapter). Most will probably not even justify the time, and money, involved in scheduling a pre-mediation meeting with the mediator. So what can you do in a simple case, a relatively modest case?

Even the story of a contract dispute can be compelling. In a dispute over a contract to buy or sell products or services, an employment agreement, a construction contract, or a loan agreement, the dispute most likely will revolve around a few key documents. Perhaps there is a written contract. Memos. Notes from meetings. A transcript of key deposition testimony. And, these days, emails!

The most effective mediator-preparation tool in my experience—and this was in a case that most observers would categorize as an ordinary business dispute—was presented in a three-ring notebook. On top of the tabbed section in the notebook was a case summary (this one was a narrative but a bullet-point, checklist style outline would have worked as well), with each factual and legal proposition in the summary supported by a footnoted reference to a key document, deposition excerpt, statute or reported decision. So Footnote 1 could be verified at Tab 1; Footnote 2 referred to Tab 2; and so forth.

Defense counsel: "We know we will win this case because there will be no evidence at trial that we owed the Plaintiff a fiduciary duty." This is the kind of assertion made during a mediation that is difficult to refute or challenge. Will there be such evidence? Yes, there will. No, there won't. Yes, there will. No, there won't.

In other words, not interesting! But thanks to excellent preparation by counsel, here's what happened next.

Me: "That's interesting (reaching for my notebook), because it seems like I read somewhere that your CEO acknowledged such a duty in his deposition. Here it is. 'Q. Mr. CEO, did you think at the time that you owed the Plaintiff a fiduciary duty? A. Well of course. I thought so at the time and still do.' "

We were able to move on to the Defendant's next point.

When used effectively, this form of pre-mediation submission allows your mediator to not only understand your position, but to advance to the next step, advocating for your position in a private caucus with your opponent.

Preparing the Client

Too often these days it seems that many lawyers are suffering the temptation to be the "good cop," keeping a cheery disposition about the case when discussing it with their client, and counting on the mediator to be the "bad cop," the deliverer of the bad news about the most likely outcomes and scenarios, about the high risk in going forward. The failure to counsel the client realistically, dimming unrealistic expectations, can become a major obstacle during a mediation.

I enjoy engaging clients in conversation throughout the process. Often, in the middle of the afternoon, I will ask a client if this is his or her first mediation. If so, I then ask, "how has the process that you have experienced so far been consistent with your mental image before you arrived this morning, and how is it different"?

While some will offer that it is what they imagined, or what their lawyer described for them, others will suggest that they never imagined it would be so tedious, or that there would be so many "back-and-forth" moves in the negotiation. But far and away the most common response is that the participant did not anticipate being separated from her adversary for most of the day; what she anticipated was across-the-table, face-to-face, direct negotiation.

Whenever I hear this I realize that this is a client who probably did not receive five minutes of preparation from her lawyer for the mediation. Because what the client anticipated is something that *never* happens.

It's easy to understand why the client may have pictured being seated across the table from her adversary throughout the process. Popular images on the nightly news of peace treaty negotiations or labor union/management negotiations often include the photo op of those participants across the table from the other. What the public doesn't see in these news accounts is that, after the camera lights were turned off, and after some brief dialogue, the negotiators in all likelihood retreated to separate conference rooms.

Preparing for the mediation means more, however, than just understanding the steps in the process. It also means having a plan, a negotiation strategy, based on your goals and an objective assessment of realistic scenarios and alternatives to settlement. If you are going to start the bidding by making the first settlement proposal at the mediation, and you think your "bottom line" is that you want to receive $100,000, should your opening demand be $500,000, $1,000,000, or $2,000,000? Should it be $150,000?

Should you try to stage the negotiation so that your opponent makes the opening proposal? If you make a demand of $2,000,000.00, is the other side going to counter with an offer of $5,000, $50,000, or just get up and leave?

Do you have goals other than monetary compensation? Do you want your old job back? Do you want the non-compete restriction waived? Do you want to pay the other side what he are owed over time, through a series of future purchase orders of their product?

The important point is simply this: *have a plan*. Anticipate the opportunity, anticipate your opponent's perspective, and consider what you can and need to do to encourage and facilitate resolution.

Preparing Your Adversary

"Will, I know that six weeks ago we sent them a demand letter for $150,000, but that was then and this is now and we want to make a demand this morning of $3,000,000."

There are no written rules in negotiation. But there are things a negotiator can do that are "unhelpful," and this is one of them!

Is the problem with the $3,000,000 demand that it is extreme, outrageous and unreasonable? Maybe, but maybe not. Perhaps in the six weeks prior to the mediation newly discovered evidence has pushed the evaluation of the case up considerably. Perhaps an important third-party witness provided some extremely helpful and unexpected deposition testimony. Perhaps the court overruled the other side's Motion for Summary Judgment, meaning the case will go before a jury. Perhaps it was learned that the Defendant, who was deemed "judgment-proof" (unable to satisfy a jury award), has just won the lottery! There can be a variety of legitimate reasons for the $3,000,000 demand.

But the problem with the $3,000,000 demand is that, by first presenting it at the mediation, the Defendant may be completely blind-sided, and caught off guard. It would not be surprising if the Defendant reasonably assumed that the negotiation would start at $150,000 and wind up at a number below that figure; the Defendant thus would have prepared accordingly. It would not be surprising if the Defendant, in response to a $3,000,000 demand, is unable or unwilling to make any offer at all. So the mediation is a bust, and time, money and other resources have been wasted.

What would have been the harm, in the week or two prior to the mediation, if the Plaintiff had sent the Defendant a revised demand, acknowledging the previous demand but explaining that at the mediation the opening demand is going to be significantly greater, and setting out the reasons for the increase?

Preparing to Win: Control the Settlement Documents

Experienced negotiators know the value in controlling the settlement documents. Being the drafter of the initial documents is a well-recognized and time-honored negotiation technique. *Why not prepare, prior to the mediation, an outline or rough draft of appropriate settlement documents, with key-provision language of your creation (confidentiality clauses, non-disparagement, releases, payment terms, indemnities, injunctive relief, etc.)* Include the draft documents with other materials for the mediator's use in your pre-mediation submission, or bring the documents on your laptop or thumb-drive to the mediation, for the mediator's use if progress is being made. If you are a lawyer, this practice will always give you an advantage in a mediation, and your client will always be impressed, because the mediator will heap praise on you effusively in the presence of your client!

Preparing settlement documents in advance fulfills another important purpose. It helps you anticipate and prepare, and it minimizes the possibility that, after a long day of negotiation when minds and bodies get worn down, you will inadvertently forget to insist on a provision that your client requires as part of any final agreement. To quote a recent Presidential candidate in a highly-publicized debate, "Oops!"

The Accident Scene Investigation

Several years ago I mediated a pedestrian intersection collision case. The nine year old Plaintiff had suffered a catastrophic brain injury. The only issue to mediate was liability. The boy had been struck by a commercial van, and there were layers of liability insurance in play. On the Sunday afternoon before the mediation, I spent 30 minutes at the intersection where the accident had occurred with the Plaintiff's lawyer, walking the intersection from all directions, and becoming familiar with the timing and sequence of the traffic lights. The accident had occurred while the mother, little boy in hand, was walking her child and a friend home from a shopping center. Their home was only a couple of blocks away. After studying the intersection, the lawyer and I paid the family a visit in their modest, but immaculate, little home. These were people dealing courageously with a horrible injury to their child. We had a nice visit. I got to know them in a way I never could have had I not been in their home, and they had a chance to get to know me, ask questions, and fully understand my role in the case.

At the mediation a few days later there were many lawyers and insurance company representatives. I was engaged in a discussion with one of the insurers who represented that his insured would not be found liable because the boy's mother, holding the child's hand, had crossed the intersection against a yellow, and then a red, light. I asked the insurer whether he had ever been to the intersection, and he said he had not. I then said, "I have. And what you are saying about the timing and sequence of the lights is not how they work." It was a key moment in the negotiation.

I like to tell this story, not because it reveals that I have some special talent as a mediator, but because it remains one of the finest examples of mediation advocacy, of anticipating the opportunity presented by a mediation and creatively preparing the mediator for it, that I have ever experienced. The case settled for $14 million, in part because the Plaintiff's counsel in that case took the time to invite me to spend a Sunday afternoon with him to really understand how the accident had occurred and who his clients were. The lawyer anticipated the opportunity and used it to maximize the result for his client.

CHAPTER 5

The Process: Do's, Don'ts and Choices

So far you have:

✓ Determined that your dispute is an appropriate one to be mediated

✓ Decided that now is as good a time as any

✓ Obtained your adversary's agreement on the selection of an experienced mediator

✓ Confirmed a date, place and time for the mediation

✓ Met with your counsel (or client) and reviewed the strengths and weaknesses of your position, and come up with a realistic negotiation strategy

✓ Submitted background materials to the mediator and had a 30 minute conference call with her

✓ Timely submitted a realistic demand letter to opposing counsel to allow her an opportunity to digest it and be prepared to respond at the mediation

The Big Day has arrived. What next?

All Together Now (Part II)

The Joint Session: The Mediator's Role

I have saved for the final chapter a discussion of a recent trend that disfavors the convening of a joint session (a meeting of all parties and counsel). Here I assume that the mediator is going to convene all the participants in a single conference room. It is my default position for every mediation, and I hope the mediator will convene a joint session at your next mediation.

Classically, the mediator summons all participants together around a conference table. The mediator makes a few remarks, perhaps reminding the participants of the ground rules, the extent to which all communication is confidential, when lunch will be arriving (very important!), and generally reviewing what to expect as the process unfolds. The goal of the mediator is to reassure the participants that they have made a wise decision in agreeing to mediate and in their selection of a mediator.

I try to make it a point in my brief remarks to remind the participants of the informality of the process. There is no script. There are no rules of procedure. Although we may break up into separate conference rooms ("private caucuses"), allowing the mediator to shuttle back and forth, there is no rule that says we have to do so. At any time the mediator may ask the lawyers to step out and engage in a discussion apart from the clients. In other circumstances, particularly when the dispute is between parties who once had a relationship, it may be appropriate to excuse counsel from the process and allow the clients to visit one-on-one, either by themselves or with the mediator present.

By introducing these ideas at the outset, a mediator is trying to encourage the participants to be open-minded, not just as to compromise and settlement, but as to the steps to be followed to get to resolution. Without previously explaining the open-ended nature of the process at the beginning, I have sometimes noticed the participants can be alarmed, if not panicked, when the mediator suddenly invites the lawyers to join him in his office for a lawyers-only discussion in the mid-afternoon. "Something must be going wrong," is the thought on their minds. So it is helpful for the mediator to reassure everyone, from the very beginning, that aside from the rule of confidentiality, there are no other rules. Like a thrill ride at the fair, the participants should be prepared for anything!

I know a popular mediator who asks each of the participants in the joint session, in turn, as she goes around the table, if he or she is attending in good faith with authority to try to reach a settlement. It is my understanding that the technique has produced positive results for her for many years, but it makes me crazy! I would have a concern that any one of the participants might answer the question with a "no," chilling the atmosphere. And since in many jurisdictions, including mine, there is no "good faith" obligation of the participants in mediation (Chapter 2 discussion), the lawyer or client who answered "no" would be perfectly within his right to do so. It seems to me that putting each participant on the spot in a joint session is inviting trouble. Which demonstrates the axiom that there are about as many styles and approaches to mediation as there are mediators.

Should the mediator ask questions and participate in the dialogue during the joint session? To a limited degree, yes. If Lawyer A makes a statement during his presentation that "such and such is undisputed," and the issue referred to strikes me as being a fairly important one, I may ask Lawyer B to confirm that the issue is, in fact, undisputed. It is also appropriate for the mediator to ask neutral questions about the procedural posture of the case (e.g., when is the discovery deadline? is there a trial setting? are there any more hearings or depositions scheduled?). There is a certain amount of efficiency in addressing these kinds of housekeeping issues in everyone's presence. I like to cover as many topics as possible while the participants are all together because it minimizes the time they will sit in their private caucus room without the mediator.

Asking questions directed to one side about the facts, law or any other matter that implies a particular view, even if the implication is just from the *tone* of the question, is strictly out of bounds. If there is a trace of a chance that someone might interpret the mere asking of the question as the taking of a position, the mediator should always err in favor of saving the question for a private caucus, and not pose it in the joint session.

But there is a purpose other than efficiency served by posing fairly generic, harmless questions in the presence of all participants. Responding to the questions may be the first unscripted, dynamic moment of the morning. In other words, everything that has occurred in the joint session up until the moment both sides have finished their presentations may very well have been scripted. Certainly the mediator's remarks are a version of remarks he gives in every mediation (I've delivered my little speech more than 3,000 times; want to hear it?) And the presentations, particularly if delivered by counsel, may actually have been rehearsed, or at least they tend to follow a fairly tight outline. So by posing questions before the parties are separated, the room is engaged in a conversation, which opens a window of opportunity for someone to unexpectedly share a piece of information that wasn't carefully packaged.

Sometimes I will deliberately ask counsel, while everyone is still together, to summarize the current status of negotiations, the status, in other words, before everyone arrived for the mediation. This question will often be posed even if I think I know the answer! There are multiple reasons for doing so.

First, one of the lawyers may have asked me to in their pre-mediation submission, because they (a) can't remember what the communication has been; (b) they have replaced prior counsel for their client in the matter, and are honestly unsure of what negotiations have previously transpired, if any; or (c) they are curious as to their opposing counsel's recollection of prior communications, and also curious if a prior offer or demand will be described as the day's starting point for negotiation, or whether there is to be a new starting point.

Second, it is not possible to exaggerate the high percentage of cases in which counsel honestly have different recollections of prior settlement communications. Here is why I say the differences are honest. Lawyers have a unique way of using hand signals, verbal cues, body language, or smoke signals in their communications with each other:

Lawyer A (while counsel are sitting in the back of the courtroom, waiting for the judge to call their matter for hearing): "Counselor, have we ever talked about trying to settle this case?"

Lawyer B: "No, I don't think so. I don't remember anything."

Lawyer A: "I didn't think so. Maybe we ought to talk about it sometime."

Lawyer B: "You're right. I've not spoken to my client about it, but I'm sure he would be willing to try to work something out. *What if* (very important words) I could get him to offer your client $50 thousand or so?"

Lawyer A: "I'm pretty sure that wouldn't be enough, but I could talk to my client about it. What do you think your client would do if my client made a demand of $100 thousand?"

Lawyer B: "I'm not sure. It sounds like way too much but . . .".

The lawyers are then summoned by the court to come forward to argue the pending motion, and the conversation is forgotten. But not *entirely* forgotten.

One year later, at the mediation, when Lawyer A's client makes an opening demand of $200,000, Lawyer B will howl in protest that "they're going UP; their last demand was $100,000!" Naturally, when Lawyer B's client initially offers $20 thousand, Lawyer A's position will surely be, "We don't get it; they've already us $50 thousand. They must be here in bad faith."

If it sounds like I've heard this conversation before it's because I've heard it *hundreds of times*. Lawyer A and Lawyer B are being honest. Although the back-bench, courtroom dialogue a year before no more included an authorized "demand" of $100 thousand any more than it did a $50 thousand "offer," our memories have a funny way of spinning things sometimes. Unfortunately, the lawyers sincerely believe that the other is engaging in whatever "bad faith" is.

Finally, there is one other thing about prior settlement negotiations that the lawyers almost certainly will disagree about, and that is *whose turn it is to make a proposal*. This is the third reason for posing this inquiry while all participants are assembled.

Like death and taxes, it can be reliably predicted that counsel will always argue that based on prior settlement discussions, it is their opponent's turn to propose something. Like the man in the TV commercials who sells men's suits and promises customer satisfaction, I guarantee it. If this sleeper issue isn't poked with a stick while the participants are all assembled, there is a very good chance that the negotiation process will bog down for an hour or two, while the lawyers argue about who is to make the next move. I am not making this up.

I have already advocated for making a pre-mediation settlement proposal, as a way to condition the other side to your dispute and to eliminate the chance that they will claim surprise and take the position that they are unable to respond. Now we see that there are two other important reasons to make a proposal in advance: it eliminates any conceivable ambiguity as to where your starting point for negotiation at the mediation will be, and it clearly places the ball in your opponent's court, requiring from them a response.

To summarize, the mediator's objective in the joint session is to facilitate communication, to set everyone at ease, and to create an atmosphere generally conducive to discussion and negotiation. This must all be accomplished in as neutral a manner as possible.

The Joint Session: Your Role

Once the mediator is done, he or she will turn to one side and say "Counsel, the floor is yours", or "Ms. Plaintiff's counsel, may I impose on you to summarize your client's perspective on things as we sit here this morning?" The floor is yielded in as neutral a manner as possible. Of course, when Party A has concluded her summary or presentation, the mediator must turn to Party B in *exactly* the same fashion, "Counsel, the floor is yours . . .", etc. A first name used in one direction must be matched by a first name used in the other. "Counsel" if used to address one side must be used to address the other. Trust me. It matters!

The custom and practice is that if the dispute is a filed lawsuit, the Plaintiff has the first opportunity to present. This tracks the normal course of trial procedure, where the Plaintiff goes first in the jury selection process, in opening and closing arguments, and the introduction of evidence. But if no suit has been filed, the question of "who presents first" can become a bit ambiguous, especially when the parties have competing claims against each other. A simple, "would anyone like to volunteer to go first," will usually work, or failing that, a coin flip!

What the parties do with the opportunity presented by a joint session is what the art of advocacy is all about.

Presentations in joint sessions range from "we're here in good faith to try to work this out" to elaborate hour-long, PowerPoint presentations, with three-ring, tabbed notebooks, flip charts, video presentations by expert or fact witnesses, key documents, maps or photos blown up on foam board, chronologies, etc.

What you decide to do with the opportunity in a joint session will be decided in your planning and preparation, and may depend on the size and complexity of the dispute, as well as your sense of who your audience will be at the mediation. Is the goal to convince opposing counsel of the strength of your legal argument, or is it to convince an insurance adjuster that your client's soft tissue injuries are real? Do you perceive that there is an opportunity to demonstrate to your adversary your degree of preparation and your readiness for trial, or do you want to poke holes in their sense of invulnerability? In any event, the joint session is a unique opportunity to communicate in an *unfiltered manner* with the client on the other side.

Keep in mind that the purpose of the joint session is not to convince the mediator of something. Feel free to ignore the mediator! Focus on the decision-maker sitting across the table from you.

Here is a trap to avoid if you are defense counsel:

Plaintiff Counsel: "Thanks to everyone for being here. I first would like to hand out our notebooks. As you can see, Tab 1 is a summary of the various witnesses whose testimony will establish liability; and Tab 2 is summary of our damage calculations, with supporting documentation. There are always facts that I, as a lawyer, wish I could change, and that is true in this case. However, we think we have a very strong case, and the fact that the Court has already overruled your Motion for Summary Judgment means we will be picking a jury in two weeks. While we are prepared for trial, we would prefer to try to work something out and avoid it. And now I would like to ask my client to say a few words about what her life has been like since the accident, and answer any questions you may have."

Defense Counsel (sitting at the conference table with a blank legal pad and nothing else): "Thanks. That was very interesting, but we're here in good faith and we would like to discuss our views with the mediator in a private caucus."

What has just happened? What does the Plaintiff (and let's presume she has never been a party to a lawsuit) think has happened? The Plaintiff thinks her lawyer is fabulous, is well prepared, knows the case inside and out, and is ready to do battle. The Plaintiff also has been given reason to believe that Defense counsel is disinterested, doesn't know the case, isn't prepared, and probably will have little to offer during the negotiations. Has this joint session made it more or less likely that the mediation will be successful? Less, but not because the mediator did a poor job or because joint sessions are a bad idea. The prospects for resolution have been reduced because of poor advocacy by Defense counsel.

Another image from the same hypothetical? Picture in your mind the previously described joint session. The defendant client representative is a local adjuster who is, personally, unfamiliar with the claim. To save travel costs, the insurer decided to send a local adjuster instead of the line adjuster with in-depth knowledge of the facts and issues in the case. The unsophisticated Plaintiff, in addition to being enthralled by her lawyer's organization and mastery of the case, notices something else. She notices that the other side does not appear to be paying attention! The "insurance company guy" across the table has his arms folded, is not taking notes, and seems to be looking out the window more than looking at anything else. The message sent? That the defendant and insurer don't care about the case, don't care about the facts, and don't really appear to care too much about anything. The defense has, unintentionally, gotten the mediation off to an unfortunate beginning.

Here is a temptation to avoid if you are plaintiff's counsel:

Plaintiff Counsel: "Mr. Defendant, now would be a good time to start being honest with your lawyer. But given the fraud that you committed here we're not sure we can reliably count on that, so we are going to share the truth with you, counsel. And the truth is that your client is a lying, cheating, scumbag. Our goal is to humiliate both of you in the courtroom."

This style of advocacy, too often seen these days, has a funny way of not resulting in a compromise and settlement!

What type of advocacy works? Consider the video and visual aids you might use to enlighten and persuade an arbitration panel, or a jury. Why not use the same resources in mediation? Consider bringing a key expert witness to the mediation, or at least utilize excerpts of videotaped expert witness testimony as part of your joint session presentation. Anticipate the opportunity. Just as you give thought to the desirable demographics you seek on your jury panel and in the jury box, give thought to who your audience will be at your next mediation. Are the other side's client representatives going to be individuals who have attended all of the depositions, all of the hearings, etc.? Or have the client representatives been absent, and presumably under-appreciate the strength and credibility of your expert's presentation? If your expert is strong and the other side's expert is weak, why not show clips of each expert "back-to-back"? The visual medium can be worth thousands of words, and millions of dollars!

The Dance

At some point the joint session will have run its course, and the mediator will split the parties up into their separate conference rooms. Where the mediator goes at that point is discretionary, but logically most mediators begin with a private caucus with the party bringing the claim, demand, or lawsuit. My practice is to allow each side a little "down time" after the joint session to unwind a bit and discuss privately with his or her counsel what just transpired.

The process of back and forth begins. To a degree, the initial stops in each caucus room are a continuation of the "information gathering" that began in the joint session. But in these initial private discussions the mediator is trying to get to know the antagonists, and get a sense of them. It is important that the mediator be a listener, during this phase, and not a talker. The dance begins with an opening demand by one party, and an opening counter by the other.

It seems like almost every day I have a Plaintiff in a mediation make an opening demand of $2,000,000, and a Defendant, perhaps an insurance company, make an opening counter-offer of $10,000. This used to make me crazy! But experience, as they say, is a great teacher, and what I have learned is that even with what would appear to be a polarized beginning, it is more likely than not that I will drive home that evening having participated in resolution of that dispute.

I don't mean to suggest that opening positions are irrelevant. You just have to learn how to deal with them, and that is why having an experienced mediator matters.

It is embarrassing now for me to reflect back on my first few hundred mediations. I am certain that what I did was take polarizing offers and demands back and forth a time or two, determine that the process was probably going to be a waste of everyone's time, and then declare an impasse and send everyone home. The irony with this early practice of premature "give-up" on my part is that it was probably one explanation for early popularity and success as a mediator! "How wonderful", the participants must have thought, "a mediator who doesn't waste everyone's time."

What I have learned is to always keep smiling, always keep nudging, and always keep encouraging the parties to stay with it. There is an excellent chance that, if the mediator refuses to give up, something will break loose and a real negotiation will begin.

I have referred to the negotiation dance and you may have heard the expression before. But what is it? Allow me to show you:

Plaintiff Demand	**Defendant Offer**
$2,000,000	
	$10,000
$1,950,000	
	$15,000
$1,910,000 ("Tell them we think we're wasting our time")	
	$18,000 ("Tell them that if they don't get serious, we are going to leave")
$1,600,000	
	$25,000 ("Tell them that if they want to see a six-figure offer, they need to get under $500,000")
$1,250,000	
	$50,000 ("This time tell them that we may or may not make any more proposals, depending on whether they get under $500,000")
$800,000 ("Tell them we've just made the biggest move of the day, and if they don't reciprocate, we're done")	
	"Tell them that we will go to $100,000 IF they will come down to $500,000" (a/k/a "a bracket")

"There is NO WAY we will go
down to $500,000. Tell them we
will go to $600,000 if they will
go to $300,000" (a "counter-
bracket")

$100,000

$500,000

$150,000

$450,000

$175,000

$300,000 ("take it or leave it")

$200,000 ("take it or leave it")

Mediator suggests the parties split the difference; case settles for
$250,000

My Feet Are Sore: Analysis

This dance usually takes hours and hours. The parties are
engaging in positional, competitive bargaining. It is risky, time-
consuming and stressful.

I think one of the most important principles of the
negotiation dance is that from time to time a negotiator needs to
give the other side a reason to hope. Even when the parties
appeared hopelessly estranged at $1.6 million and $25 thousand,
the Defendant referred to a six-figure offer, easing the Plaintiff's
concern that the Defendant might not be prepared to even go to
$100,000. And although the Plaintiff's demands were excessive,
and Plaintiff wasn't adhering to the Defendant's requirements, at
least the Plaintiff was making some large moves in response to

relatively small moves by the Defendant, encouraging the Defendant to just stay the course and see where it lead.

At $800 thousand vs. $50 thousand, the Defendant proposed a "bracket." A bracket is any version of "I'll do A, if you'll do B". Brackets are often very effective at closing large gaps. If you are in a negotiation and the difference between the parties is $60 thousand vs. $50,000, you don't need a bracket. The negotiation is already "bracketed." But when the parties in our hypothetical were at $800 thousand vs. $50,000, a bracket made sense.

A bracket is essentially a face-saving way for a negotiator to make a larger move than he or she would otherwise. In our example, the Defendant proposed a bottom bracket of $100 thousand. This was not in line with the progression of the Defendant's prior moves. It was twice the Defendant's previous offer of $50 thousand, and twice the size of the Defendant's previous, largest adjustment (from $25 thousand to $50 thousand). But the face-saving aspect of the bracket is that the Defendant coupled the large move with a condition, a condition that the Plaintiff move from $800 thousand to $500 thousand.

While the Plaintiff's response to the condition was not "o.k.", the Plaintiff's counter was substantial enough to keep the negotiation energized.

Another recurring practice of some experienced negotiators is to remain mindful of the midpoint between the positions of the two parties. Some negotiators are almost obsessed with a mid-point analysis, and will never deviate from a negotiation path that always leaves them with a midpoint that would be satisfactory. Other negotiators are less interested in the midpoint, and prefer to focus on the bottom line.

Finally, there is one thing a mediator should always be mindful of if the parties seem to be interested in nothing other than hurling insults at each other. No one has gone home. In my mind I am always thinking, "if these people are as offended as they say they are by the other side's position, why don't they leave?" As long as both sides are still present anything can happen.

Interest-Based Negotiation

The "back and forth" detailed above, a negotiation that had a happy ending, is a classic example of the negotiation dance. Although the method worked, it is also a classic example of positional or competitive bargaining, which often is risky, confrontational and ultimately unsuccessful. It is because the mediator is always exploring the parties' interests, and not just their positions, that the mediator's role is often crucial to the outcome.

Getting to Yes, a phenomenal little book and a New York Times best-seller, was published by two Harvard professors in 1981. *Getting to Yes* introduced the general public to interest-based negotiating. One way the authors explain the meaning of interest-based negotiation is to describe two young children fighting over an orange. "I want it." "No, I saw it first, give it to me." And on and on. In this story the authors describe the typical adult who happens upon the scene, cannot tolerate the bickering and squabbling, grabs the orange, cuts it in half, and gives each child half of the orange. The adult then witnesses the children separating, with one child peeling the orange and eating the meat of the orange, and the other child peeling the orange and playing with the peel. The lesson? If the adult had bothered to ask the children *why* each of them wanted the orange, there is a chance that each child would have ended up 100% satisfied. Each child's *position* was they wanted the orange, but each child's *interest* was something different. *Getting to Yes* is a classic, and a must read for any negotiator.

A car salesman's *position* is the quoted price of the car. But a car salesman has many interests: having a happy customer; having a happy sales manager; get the best price possible relative to the price at which the dealership has sold other versions of the same model; closing a sale that very day for month-end quota purposes; etc.

A car buyer's *position* is the dollar amount offered for the car. But the buyer has many interests, as well: making certain she gets a good value; making sure she doesn't find out that a neighbor or friend at church got the same car for a thousand dollars less; maintaining a good relationship with the dealership where the car will be serviced; closing the sale quickly because she is tired of looking at cars; etc.

In our negotiation dance, the positions of the parties were their stated demands (or offers) of money. But what might have been their interests?

Plaintiffs' interests: usually "fairness," reflected in a notion that they don't want to settle for less than the full value of their claim (sometimes defined as what someone else received for a similar claim); payment sooner (21 days) rather than later (2 years); avoiding having to be deposed, or avoiding having to be cross-examined on the witness stand in the courtroom; saving family members and friends the same burden of testifying; not having to reveal publicly their employment, marital, health or educational history; a desire for privacy and confidentiality or, conversely, a desire for public attention and publicity; avoiding any additional attorney's fees and other costs of disputing.

Defendants' interests: "fairness" (sometimes defined as not paying any more than legally obligated to pay); hanging on to the money as long as possible; avoid being deposed or having friends, family or business associates deposed; avoid business disruption; avoid adverse publicity; avoid settling, which might encourage a long line of similarly situated former employees or customers to bring claims; avoid unnecessary attorney's fees and costs.

The more you brainstorm the interests of the two sides in a negotiation, the more likely it is that you will discover that some of the interests are mutual and overlapping. While the parties and their lawyers are engaged in positional, competitive bargaining, the mediator is constantly exploring the interests of both sides, in an effort to achieve as mutually advantageous a resolution of the matter as possible.

Changing the Dynamics

It was previously mentioned that a mediator may suggest the possibility during the joint session of a client-to-client dialogue at some point in the process. I have learned that planting this seed early on in the process can be productive.

Too often disputes arise out of mutually productive and satisfactory relationships that fail. Whether the dispute is between an architect and contractor, or employer and employee, or distributor and retailer, or husband and wife, at some point there may be a breakdown in communication, and then trust, and the relationship fails. One side sends a demand letter to the other. The other hires a lawyer who responds. Suddenly both sides are lawyered-up and litigation ensues. Perhaps a year or two goes by. Depositions, motions, hearings, document production. All the while the parties are paying money to their lawyers, and the lawyers are instructing their clients not to do business with, or even communicate with the other side.

And then everyone appears at the mediation.

Mediator: "Ms. Plaintiff, I'm curious. I know this lawsuit has been going on for over a year. When's the last time you ever sat down and spoke directly with the knucklehead down the hall (the Defendant) about how this all got started and so forth."

Plaintiff: "Oh my goodness. That was a long time ago. It's probably been about 18 months. And it's a shame all of this has happened, because we used to get along quite well. Our families even used to take trips together."

Mediator: "We're probably going to be here all day. But if you think there would be any value in just the two of you sitting down in a room together and talking this through, let me know."

I have been mediating for years and years, and I can promise you that there is one response the client in this dialogue has almost each and every time.

Plaintiff: "You mean, we could do that?"

In other words, the parties have become locked in by their own mindset or their lawyer's direction to being a party to a lawsuit, and part of that mindset is that you can never speak or otherwise communicate with the enemy. And when the possibility of something so simple as setting up a conversation between two people is raised, there often is a moment of genuine disbelief!

For this conversation to occur the consent of both parties, and of both counsel, is required. But I find that more often than not the parties are eager for the opportunity.

As I gather the clients together for this private conversation, I stand at the door of the conference room they will be using and I ask them to consider three things: (1) this case belongs to them and not their lawyers; (2) they should take all the time in the world to have this conversation and not worry about those of us outside the room-we'll find something to do; and (3) the purpose of mediation is to make the mediator look good with the judge, so I would appreciate it if they would stay focused and try to help me out (this little joke never fails to break the ice, which is what I want, of course).

Each and every time, and I mean EACH and EVERY time, as I close the door on these disputing parties, one of them will say to the other, "Well, at least we would both like to quit paying our lawyers!" There is laughter and the door clicks shut, and I am certain that something good is going to come from their meeting.

It was my early experience as a mediator that the idea of letting the clients visit on their own would usually come up at the end of the day, perhaps as an impasse was being declared, and the participants were packing their things, preparing to go get in their cars and return to their homes, offices, airports, or hotels. It would occasionally happen that someone, perhaps me but perhaps one of the lawyers or one of the clients would say, "Would there be any harm before we leave in letting the clients visit?" In this early experience, when these conversations would occur in the late afternoon or early evening, invariably the clients would emerge from their meeting to announce they had either settled the dispute, or at least achieved a basis for further negotiation and not impasse. I began to wonder: *why are we always saving these opportunities for the end of the day when all else has failed? Why not look for these opportunities early in the process, perhaps sparing everyone the hard feelings that go with polarizing positions that are a hallmark of the process?*

Writing on a Stone Table: The MSA

In many jurisdictions a handshake is insufficient to enforce a settlement agreement. If an agreement can be achieved during the mediation, it should be reduced to writing and signed by the parties.

Though some may disagree, I consider it a best practice as mediator to draft a "one-pager", a Mediated Settlement Agreement ("MSA"). Those who disagree take the view that drafting an MSA is fraught with peril, and amounts to advocacy, which the neutral should strictly avoid. I disagree. I will usually begin this task as I am going back and forth between the parties when I begin to sense that a settlement is likely. The parties and their counsel are presented with my draft, and invited to edit and add to it to their heart's content. It is important that a mediator's draft not be perceived to be a recommendation, but merely a service being provided by the mediator to facilitate a final agreement.

In my state it is recommended that the MSA include an expression of the parties' intent to be bound by the MSA, notwithstanding that more elaborate settlement documents are contemplated. Should a dispute arise over the final documents at some later date, this expression makes it virtually certain that a court will enforce the MSA if requested by one party to do so.

Over the years I have become fond of suggesting that there appears to be a direct correlation between the height of a building that a lawyer offices in, and the amount of editing they want to do to my draft of the MSA! In other words, if a lawyer offices in a sixty-story building, it is likely that he or she is going to want to practically re-write the MSA; if the lawyer offices in a one or two story building, they are usually fine with what I put in front of them. This always gets a laugh, in part, I think, because there is a kernel of truth to it!

So providing the parties with a draft of an MSA is a "best practice" for mediators, but don't forget that a best practice for advocates is to draft a settlement document prior to arriving for the mediation, as was discussed in the previous chapter.

One way or the other, it is wise not to let the parties get away without a written agreement, signed by all parties.

Every mediation is a unique event. The personalities of the parties, counsel, and the mediator will influence the dynamics of any mediation just as surely as the facts involved in the dispute being mediated. Anticipate the opportunity, prepare, and approach the process with an open mind, and the process can reward you with resolution.

It Wasn't About the Money

Almost every day someone in a mediation tries to convince me that, "it's not about the money". "Will, the money doesn't matter, the point is that they screwed with me, and now they're going to pay." "Will, I don't care about the money, they hurt my reputation."

No matter what they say, it nearly always turns out to be about the money. But not every time.

A venture-capital start-up in Houston was created with the goal of cornering the world oil market with remarkable new drilling equipment. I'm never very good on the technical details.

The new company invited a young member of a Middle Eastern royal family to join the board. We will call him "Omar." Omar's role was to introduce the company to the Prime Minister of OPEC, the head of the Argentinian oil company, and other friends of the family. Omar's uncles, apparently, were disapproving of the idea, something about the way Americans do business, and they counseled the young man to reject the invitation.

Omar couldn't resist. The young oil guru joined the board of directors, and for whatever reason signed a modest consulting agreement that would pay him a stipend of $10,000 per month for five years of his service.

As fate would have it, the company's fortunes went flat, and about two years into the arrangement a new wave of venture capital had to be rounded up to sustain the business. With the new investment came a new board of directors. Out with the old, in with the new. Bye, bye, Omar.

Tail between his legs, Omar headed home. But at some point Omar realized, "hey, they owe me that $10,000 per month for about three more years." Lawsuit. Mediation.

I wanted to be Omar. Omar flew his own jet. His handsomeness was exceeded only by his charm, sense of humor and intelligence. Omar had been educated at the finest schools, and his manners were impeccable. And Omar was freakishly wealthy.

"Mr. Pryor, when they excused me from the board, they dishonored me and they dishonored my family. It is not about the money." There could not be a trace of a doubt about the truth of his statement. Omar exuded sincerity; his feelings had been hurt; he had been embarrassed. Nor could I overlook the fact that somewhere over the Atlantic Ocean, on his way to attend the mediation in Texas, the cost of the fuel consumed by Omar's *private jet probably surpassed the modest amount of the dollars at issue in the lawsuit.*

Let's remember the lessons from Getting to Yes. Omar's position in the mediation was that he wanted money, and his position was communicated as a demand for monetary payment. But Omar's interests were varied: he wanted to "win," he wanted the other side to be proven wrong, he wanted to salvage something that might impress his family, but most importantly, Omar wanted to save face.

So how was the matter resolved? No money was exchanged, but the company, upon my suggestion, extended a personal, face-to-face invitation to Omar to rejoin the board. I knew that Omar did not want to be on the board. No, Omar just wanted to be invited to rejoin. So Omar graciously declined, and everyone shook hands.

I still want to be Omar.

CHAPTER 6

What Do You Mean "It Didn't Work"? Following Through

If you ever watch golf on TV, you may notice that the announcers can go on and on about a golfer's swing. And I mean "on and on"! One aspect of the swing they seem particularly obsessed with is the follow-through. Does the golfer finish with his hands high, or his hands low? Did he turn the face of the club after impact? Did he maintain club head speed beyond the point of contact? Did his hips finish aligned with or facing the target? Did his right-heel come off the ground? Like I said, on and on.

I have spent a lifetime watching golf and wondering how anything could possibly matter in terms of the result of the swing that occurs after the point of impact with the ball. I mean, after the ball leaves the face of the club, how could it possibly matter where the golfer's hands, hips, or heel wind up? Perhaps this explains why I am not very good at golf!

The follow-through is important to the golf swing, and it is vitally important to the mediator's game, as well. Believe it or not, not every negotiation dance has a happy ending! The process can, and often will, result in an impasse, when no more movement by either of the negotiators will occur.

What then?

Bored? Not for Long

In the previous chapter we discussed one time-honored method of breaking an impasse, the one-on-one client meeting designed to change the dynamics of the negotiation dance. In fact, there are a number of things that can be done to change the dynamics of a mediation. A day-long mediation, when the process has followed the traditional pattern of back-and-forth shuttling between the conference rooms by the mediator, will often achieve a certain rhythm. This rhythm, as long as it is facilitating movement by the negotiators and progress towards resolution, is a good thing. But just as the Sunday afternoon golf tournament on TV can produce a sort of complacency (ever notice how they will replay a putt that you just saw roll into the cup *in slow motion*, from several angles, including a grass-level camera? now there's excitement!), the rhythm of mediation can result in a sort of lethargy amongst all of the participants. If you are engaged in a process that is not working, change the process.

Introducing the clients to a new conference room without counsel present is a way of changing the process. Just as often, having counsel step out and visit together with the mediator and without the clients present is another way of changing the process.

There are other ways. At my office complex there is a substantial water feature that wraps around a couple of office buildings and a major hotel between them, complete with pathways, fountains, trees and benches, and occasionally ducks! On more than one occasion, when the weather has been right, changing the dynamics has meant taking one of the parties for a walk around this pool. Fresh air. A change of scenery. A fresh perspective.

Did Anyone Bring a Corkscrew?

Several years ago I attended a very high-toned conference for experienced mediators sponsored by the Straus Institute for Dispute Resolution at Pepperdine University in Malibu, California. The Straus Institute is about as good as it gets in the field of continuing education in the ADR world, and on this day our luncheon speaker was a mediator from Los Angeles who, we were told, was pretty much the most popular mediator in L.A., and L.A., in turn, one of the hottest ADR markets in the country. Anyway, she was an exceptional speaker, at times mesmerizing, and she spoke without notes. I know I learned a lot from her presentation, and later I learned that nearly everyone at the conference had the same high opinion of her that I did. But this mediator-presenter had a way of changing the dynamics of a mediation that I had not, until then, thought of.

It was explained to us that her daily fee was $10,000 (this was enough years ago that it might be twice that by now!), and this bit of information alone had all of the mediators in the room on the edge of their seats, listening intently. She added that during her mediations, at 4:00 in the afternoon, regardless of what was happening in the mediation, everything was stopped-down for a *wine tasting*, "and for $10,000, I'm not talking about the kind of wine most of you probably buy at the grocery store." Forgetting about the obvious condescension in her tone (I turned to the fellow next to me and whispered, "how did she know I buy my wine at the grocery store?"), I recognized that what she was describing was one way of changing the dynamics and lightening the mood of her mediation participants, in what I am sure was a very classy manner. Would the introduction of alcohol into the mediation practice work for me, in my market? I don't think so. The important lesson is that I am sure that what she was doing, and the way she did it, was effective for her.

Other mediators may have their own personalized techniques for creating movement in a stalled negotiation. I know mediators who have the capability of baking cookies in their office suite, and I am told that the scent of the cookies in the oven, by itself, can cause a negotiation to loosen up. Popcorn? I've heard of that one, too. Any experienced mediator will tell you that how lunch is catered, and what drinks and snacks are made available to the participants, can make a great deal of difference to a successful outcome.

Fore!

While we are still on the subject of golf, I was a golfer at one point in time, and just for fun and marketing purposes I ordered several cases of golf balls, imprinted with my little logo. Sometimes, when a client was using a putter and putting toy that I have in each of my conference rooms, I would mention that when cases settled I would give out a sleeve of these logo golf balls to each of the participants. Again, in the beginning of this practice of giving away golf balls I thought I was only doing it for a) marketing, and b) fun. But I soon learned that *people who play golf love to get sleeves of free, logo golf balls*. Next I learned that they love the gift of these golf balls so much that they will do irrational things, like pay more money or accept less money to settle a case at mediation than they were prepared to otherwise, *just to ensure that they do not walk out at the end of the day without a sleeve of balls*. Is this crazy? Absolutely. Am I making this up? Absolutely not!

I am not a golfer these days (and those golf balls were expensive!), so I no longer have any to give away. But like every experienced mediator, I have other tricks.

Do These Windows Open?

It was a wonderful thing when years ago "business casual" became the law of the land, allowing mediators and mediation participants to dress comfortably on a regular basis. Until that glorious moment I made a habit of wearing a suit each day for the mediation. One day, as I was going back and forth between conference rooms, I realized that I was a little warm, so as I passed my office I removed my coat and left it on the back of a chair. Upon then entering a conference room I heard one participant say, "the mediator thinks we're going to be here for awhile—he removed his coat." I started to react by explaining that, no, I was just a bit warm, but then I thought the better of it. A couple of weeks later the scenario repeated itself and I was struck with this lesson learned: *there will be cases when, regardless of my discomfort through the afternoon, I should not remove my coat because I need to save that event for a moment in the process when I will need a visual cue to encourage the parties*!

Indiana Jones Would Like This

In a previous chapter we learned about the value of preparing a Mediated Settlement Agreement ("MSA"). But additional value from having an MSA in the works as a negotiation dance winds down is the ability to use it, like coat removal, as a visual cue.

Experienced mediators are accustomed to being scrutinized during the back-and-forth process by the participants in each room. Whether the mediator is cheerful or gloomy, upbeat or solemn, friendly or distracted, will instantly be observed upon entering each conference room, and the negotiators in the room will read into even a microscopic observation what they will.

As I go back and forth I ordinarily have a three-ring notebook in my hands. The notebook is, of course, for note-taking as well as keeping a few pertinent documents handy. If for the first time in a long day of going back-and-forth I do not have the notebook in my hands, someone in the room will always notice and point it out. "He doesn't have his notebook. What does it mean? Does this mean we're done?"

If during the back and forth process I have stepped into my office to begin generating an MSA, sometimes I will print it out, roll it up and carry it nonchalantly into a conference room like a baton. As the normal dialogue ensues, the latest demand, the latest offer, etc., I will be sure to be casual about the baton in my hand, as if it would be just fine if no one notices it. But someone always does. "What's that in your hand?", comes the inquiry. "Oh this?", I say, holding it up as if I had forgotten I had it. "This is just a one-page settlement agreement that I've generated. If we can get to an agreement I like to have something ready to go, because it will be in everyone's interest to sign something." The client's interest in this baton I have now rolled out on the conference table is palpable. "I've provided spaces for each party's signature, but other than that, there's just this one blank left to fill in."

The client can barely stand it. The dispute has been going on for a year or two. Disputing has been stressful on the business and on the family. The dispute has been draining cash reserves and savings accounts, and the courts being what they are, the client knows the end is not near. An appeal, no matter what happens at trial, is certain. Years of delay and sleepless nights are certain, as well.

The baton has now become the legendary map that leads to the Holy Grail. Resolution of the dispute and getting it over with, for months a concept that seemed so abstract, is now real. The piece of paper is tantalizing. Just a couple of signatures, and like magic, a new life can begin!

A Good Kind of Pit Bull

The best mediators, the most popular mediators in every market are the ones who never give up, even after it has become necessary to declare an impasse and send everyone home. Survey after survey support two conclusions about the attitude of regular mediation participants: a) the thing they like the least about mediation is the chatty mediator whose remarks to begin the joint session go on-and-on, longer even than a golf broadcaster's swing analysis; and b) the thing they appreciate the most about mediation is a tenacious mediator, one who never quits.

As a mediator you should make it a habit of using a reminder system to nudge you thirty, sixty or ninety days after an impassed mediation to get in touch with both sides with a phone call or email. "Just checking in, any developments?" "When we were together in April it seems we couldn't make progress because of a motion pending with the court. Did it ever get ruled on?" "Has anything happened? Have there been any more negotiations?" "Can you think of anything I can do at this point to be helpful?"

Who is not going to appreciate an overture like that? Sometimes the mere stirring of the pot will cause a dialogue, and a negotiation, to resume. There will be times in this kind of communication with one party when you will learn that the party would actually be willing to re-convene the mediation but is unwilling to voice that interest with the other side. The party wants to know if there is a face-saving way for you, as mediator, to get the parties back together. Not every time, of course, but as often as not, the mediator can get a similar expression of interest from the other side, and in the blink of an eye the parties are back at the negotiation table. It wouldn't have happened but for the mediator's follow-up.

We strategically removed the coat, we baked the cookies, we sipped the wine, we offered up the golf balls, we rolled out the baton, we followed up thirty days later, and . . . nothing.

Now what?

Time for a mediator's proposal.

When All Else Fails: "Yes" or "No"!

You, the reader, are probably getting itchy for another nostalgic look back at when my children were young, so here you go.

When my youngest child was in kindergarten, my mediation practice was still getting legs so I was blessed with being able to pick her up at the end of the school day and drive her home on many occasions. Along with my asking about her day, her classmates, and her teacher, she developed the friendly habit of asking me, "Daddy, did you have a mediation today?" (Although it was pronounced "mee-ji-a-shun"). If I said yes she would follow up with "Tell me about Party A and Party B." I could never figure out how much she was following along, but just in case, I would disguise the case if it involved a subject matter that I did not want to go remotely near by saying, "it was just a boring insurance case." I am certain that she was clueless as to what "insurance" was, but she finally learned to say, "Tell me about Party A and Party B, or was it just a boring insurance case?" Those were fun times.

Anyway, we went through this patterned dialogue one afternoon, and I explained that one party wanted one dollar, but the other side only wanted to pay fifty cents, and from her little car seat behind me I get this: "Why didn't they just split it?" I nearly ran off the road!

I do not make this stuff up.

Inevitably there will be impasses when, as the mediator, you are certain that there is still an opportunity for resolution. You know, either because a party told you or simply because you are experienced with how the process works, that at least one of the parties still has room to move. In fact, you may know that both sides have room left to negotiate. So why won't they?

Why do we have wars?

Let's say Party A, after a day of dancing, declares, "Our bottom line is $100,000. Mr. Mediator, that is a 'take it or leave it.' We have a plane to catch so the other side had better decide in a hurry." Party B: "We came here today with a plan to try to settle for anything under $75,000. Tell Party A that we said $80,000, take it or leave it, and they can go catch their plane. We don't care."

Sometimes negotiators make statements like "take it or leave it" and "bottom line" and "final proposal" and it turns out the statement is true. But sometimes it turns out that the statement wasn't necessarily true. Or maybe it was true when uttered, but the party making the statement has a change of heart, or a change of mind.

In any event, let's assume that in our hypothetical the parties meant what they said. Impasse at $100,000 vs. $80,000.

The next day (or the next week, this is not science), you as the mediator send the lawyers on each side a proposal. "Counsel, thank you for your patience, professionalism and good humor throughout our recent mediation. I regret that we were not successful in bringing this matter to resolution. I thought it would do no harm to offer the following proposal." A deadline for responding is included, usually twenty-four hours, but longer if you think one side is going to need more time. In my proposal letters I ask the parties to respond, regardless of whether the response is positive or negative. The letter includes this critically important reassurance: *"You have my guarantee that if your client is willing to accept the proposal, and the other side does not, the other party will never learn from me that you accepted."* Following the proposal itself is a set of boxes for each lawyer to check and a space for their signatures. The boxes are labeled, "YES" and "NO."

The guarantee is what allows the technique to work in most instances. It is simply stunning to learn how common it is for a party to a negotiation to be willing to make one more adjustment in his negotiation position on the condition that his adversary never learns of the acceptance unless the case settles. The mediator's proposal is a face-saving technique that allows many disputes that impassed at the end of the mediation session to be settled.

In my hypothetical I will allow you one guess as to what I would propose. You are, no doubt, correct. Now I will allow you one guess at the odds of receiving two "yes" responses to a mediator proposal in the hypothetical of $90,000! The correct answer is darn near 100% of the time!

Mediator proposals should not be attempted after every impasse. One concern with doing so routinely is that clever negotiators will learn to "negotiate to an impasse," and then wait for the proposal to split the difference. There is risk in the mediator proposal solution, so negotiating to a final settlement at the mediation is a far more advisable method to rely upon. Another concern with making proposals too often is the risk itself. The mediator has only one arrow in his or her quiver, and if the arrow doesn't hit its mark, the mediator usually has no options left.

Naturally, I used a hypothetical that would be easy. This is, after all, a short *and happy* guide to mediation! What if the impasse at mediation was $50,000 vs. $15,000, or $3,000,000 vs. $100,000? Mediators should attempt proposals only when there appears to be a reasonable prospect of success. Car-seat wisdom aside, the mediator's proposal is not always a simple matter of proposing a split-the-difference solution. I have settled a case with a proposal where the mediation reached an impasse of Party A demanding payment from Party B of $100,000, and Party B demanding payment from Party A of some lesser amount, by proposing that the parties agree to a "mutual walkaway" (no money, just mutual releases). In the challenging hypothetical above, at $50,000 vs. $15,000, the proposal might be $20,000, $25,000, or $35,000.

Is a mediator's proposal a recommendation by the mediator? I try to be clear that my proposals are not recommendations. Even as a highly evaluative mediator ("if you try your case 10 times, I don't see you being successful more often than 3 times"), I feel that when a mediator makes a recommendation, he or she has crossed the line of neutrality, and is engaging in advocacy. So the proposal is not always a dollar amount that splits the difference, nor something the mediator need deem a fair solution; it is just something that the mediator thinks might draw two "yes" responses.

In highly unusual circumstances, and only when requested to do so by both sides, I have turned a proposal into a recommendation, with an explanation as to why I thought it was in the best interest of both sides to say "YES."

It seems the timing of a mediator's proposal can make as much difference to the outcome as the terms of the proposal itself.

At the end of a long negotiation dance, when it appears that an impasse is inevitable, one or both sides may begin to sense that the most likely scenario for salvaging the opportunity and reaching an agreement is a mediator's proposal. One or sometimes both lawyers will suggest that the proposal be made on the spot, with all participants still in attendance. "Will, we have everyone here, and everyone is focused." "If you don't do it now, we will lose all the momentum we have achieved. People will get away and change their minds. It's now or never!" Believe me, I've heard the arguments for the "right then and there" proposal.

But I won't do it. I have had lawyers beg me to do it, and then shake their heads in disgust when I wouldn't.

Of course, what I really mean is I won't do it "on the spot" *unless I have to.* Is it Friday evening and has the case been called to trial and jury selection on Monday morning? Is a deposition of an extremely expensive expert witness scheduled for the following morning, and could the dollars spent on that expert be the dollars needed to get a "YES" response to the proposal? Is there any other circumstance that makes resolution on the spot imperative?

Because otherwise, I make the parties go get in their cars or cabs, and go home, go to the airport, or go back to their hotel, disappointed and frustrated and angry at the mediation process and the mediator. I want the parties to go back to their families and jobs, reflecting on their disappointment and frustration.

I'm not mean, I just know what I'm doing!

If I succumb to the pressure and do a mediator's proposal on the spot (each side is presented the proposal, and given 15 or 20 minutes to give me an answer), the success rate is around 25%. If I make the parties go home, etc., the success rate of doing a mediator proposal is around 90%. Once again I'm afraid that I win the argument because this is a fact, not opinion!

What *is* an opinion is why this discrepancy is so profound. I believe it is because when I have spent a long day at a negotiation table with someone who has absolutely worn themselves out trying to convince me of his "bottom line," it violates his integrity to put his in a position, while we are still in each other's presence, to admit that his bottom line was not, in reality, a bottom line. When the person can escape to home or office, the option offered by a mediator's proposal can be fully realized.

When all else fails, desperate times call for desperate measures. I have participated in coin flips to see who got the "win" in an impasse over $5,000. I have negotiated the rules for a one-on-one basketball game (no dunking!) to close out a similar negotiation between two men, both of whom were former college basketball players, disputing over an employment agreement. And I have facilitated a negotiation over a substantial charitable gift to a hospital, which was the only consideration for a settlement that had absolutely nothing to do with healthcare or the hospital.

Mediation works, and that is why it is not going away.

Candid Camera

Nancy leaned back in her office chair, and stared at the ceiling. "Wait a minute", she thought after a moment or two. "What's that?"

Nancy took off her shoes and got up on her desk. Standing, she was able to reach the overhead light fixture, which had a feature she had not noticed before. Turns out it was a hidden camera.

After asking a few questions, Nancy learned that her school district employer's version of why there was a hidden camera over her desk went like this: Nancy shared her office with some file cabinets; some of the file cabinets contained sensitive files including student grades, achievement results, test scores, etc.; other administrators in the school administration office, besides Nancy, had access to the file cabinets; in recent months the district had started to experience a security breach with respect to the files—files were turning up missing; district security officials had recommended monitoring the office with a hidden surveillance camera.

For days this explanation bothered Nancy. Why had no one told her about the camera? Weren't there other, less-invasive ways to address a security concern before installing a camera? Then it dawned on her. Most of her co-workers were well aware that a couple of days a week, before leaving the office to go work out at her gym on the way home, Nancy would close the door to her office and change into her workout clothes.

Now Nancy was really bothered.

Litigation ensued. There were three defendants, the school-district employer, a private security firm hired by the school district, and a firm that had subcontracted to provide and install the camera. Each defendant was represented at the mediation by counsel, by a client representative, by a liability insurance carrier representative, and in two instances, by insurance coverage counsel. Nancy had two very fine lawyers in attendance. In other words, we had a crowd.

As they often do, things proceeded well and normally. We had a joint session where all were convened and each party had a chance to share respective positions and concerns with the group. Things continued to proceed normally into the first few rounds of the negotiation dance, as I shuttled between the four conference rooms full of participants.

But as the day wore on some of the participants began to lose what I will call their "professional edge," and the appropriate conduct, demeanor and overall professionalism that had been abundant early in the morning began to unravel. This is not uncommon, but on this day, the deterioration became alarming. Eventually, various participants, including the lawyers, in private caucuses, began to refer to Nancy as a "bitch" and a "slut." It turns out Nancy had experienced, before she became a mature and well-educated school administrator, a few walks on the "wild side."

Things deteriorated to such an extent that I reconvened everyone except Nancy and her lawyers. By now the defendants and their counsel and representatives had reached such a state of agitation that they were visibly angry, spewing senseless garbage about how they were going to "tear Nancy a new one" when she got on the witness stand at trial.

The technique is sometimes referred to as "holding up a mirror." I asked the group to calm down, look in the mirror, and think about what was reflected in it. I suggested that their obvious contempt for Nancy was not attractive or appealing, and that I thought it unlikely that they would be able to disguise their contempt and disgust for Nancy in a courtroom. Finally, I suggested what might happen to them if one or more of the jurors were not appreciative of their contempt for Nancy.

There were about fifteen people in the room listening to my gentle hand-slapping. One of them was an insurance company representative from Chicago who had not said much of anything all day. Out of the corner of my eye, I noticed that he was in the back of the room, his chair tilted up against the wall. I made eye contact with him for a split second, and he nodded.

A few minutes later it was evident that no more progress would be made that day, and I declared an impasse. On his way out the door, the insurance rep handed me his card and said, "call me."

I waited a day or two and then called him. It turns out that he had been as offended and shocked as I had by the conduct of the others on his team at the mediation. He agreed with me that the failure of the professionals to remain objective could lead to dire consequences. We discussed the possibility of a mediator's proposal. I told him what I thought might be Nancy's bottom dollar. He asked me to do a mediator's proposal at that number, split responsibility for it three ways among the three defendants, and provide for a week-long deadline to give him time to make calls; he promised me he would work on it.

The deadline for responding to the proposal was 12:00 noon on the following Friday. I knew that everyone would be assembled in one lawyer's conference room at 1:00 pm on that day for a last-minute deposition. What was estimated to be a two-week jury trial would begin the following Monday.

The final "yes" response of four "yes" responses arrived at 12:45 pm. I called the lawyers office where the deposition was being convened, and was put on a speaker phone. I advised the group that they could all go home, because the case was settled.

I then called the court administrator to advise her that they could remove Nancy's case from the docket, and call someone else's case to trial on Monday.

The story is about following through. Mediations don't have to end when everyone goes home. Sometimes the moment that everyone is assembled is just not the right moment, but the parties still need a neutral facilitator to bring them together. Mediators can and should stay on the case. Nudge, nudge, nudge. Persistence matters, and persistence is often rewarded.

CHAPTER 7

What's Wrong with the Process These Days, and How Can We Fix It?

The virtues of mediation are sung by a chorus across this great land, but the practice of mediation has developed some warts. We have come a long way from the "village elder" image of mediation, to the commercial, profitable practice of mediation today. Mediation can be fairly characterized as a growth industry. A few short decades ago mediation wasn't any sort of industry, at all. So growing pains have been inevitable, and deserve our attention.

Even a "short and happy" guide to mediation must address a cultural phenomenon I will refer to as "too much mediation." Has the use of mediation become, in a sense, too popular? As mediation began taking hold in the 1980's and into the 1990's, no advocate of ADR in general and mediation in particular, could have envisioned what the practice of mediation in many markets has become. Nor would many pioneers in the field of ADR say that today there is not a need for some course correction. *The essence of mediation, the reason for mediation, is to assist parties to a dispute to achieve resolution of that dispute. Has the commercialization of mediation in recent years moved us away from what mediation has always been about? Occasionally the answer to the question has to be "yes."*

In my home state our legislature passed an "Alternative Dispute Resolution Procedures Act" in 1987, which states up front that it is the policy of my state "to encourage the peaceable resolution of disputes." The statute goes on to provide a bare bones list of what "alternative" methods of dispute resolution are contemplated—mediation being the only one of true significance—and then grants courts throughout the state the discretion to refer pending lawsuits to mediators. The statute is simple, and its purpose is unequivocally laudatory.

Who would have imagined that twenty-five years later courts in the highest population areas of my state would adopt standard, computerized scheduling orders that include a mediation referral for *every case* on the docket? Would the founders of the ADR movement not be surprised to learn that, after decades of referrals, some courts have become addicted to mediation referral as a means of docket control, and some judges require litigants to mediate over and over again? I have mediated matters in which I learned that the parties had already mediated four or five times. In these circumstances there can come a point when one of the litigants begins to figure out that the Court is never going to allow their case to be tried, so they "roll over" and give up their claim or defense. When the mediator reports to the court that the matter has settled, it is easy to anticipate the Court's reaction: mediation worked again! This practice is abusive; it is an unintended consequence of an overall experience leading to too much of a good thing. As an amateur cook, I have learned through trial and error to avoid the temptation of thinking "if a little bit of this spice is good, a lot more must be better." Perhaps this a lesson for our courts with respect to their referral practices.

Who would have imagined, in the late 1980's, that national mediation firms would develop and compete with each other, and that some communities would include dozens or more full-time dispute resolution professionals. *I never cease to be amazed that I enjoy a professional practice that did not exist when I was in law school.*

While mediation is often described as a "win-win" opportunity, a chance for both sides in a dispute to come away satisfied, there is a better-than-zero chance, if you are an experienced mediation participant, that you have become disenchanted with the process, or at least had a recent experience that left you shaking your head. The multiple referrals to mediation of a single case, the referral of cases over the objections of the parties, or a court's referral of a case that has no realistic prospect of settling, are all symptoms of a something being askew.

Too Much Mediation?

There are other manifestations of what I consider to be the "too much mediation" syndrome:

- ✓ too many mediations scheduled on a "half-day" basis;

- ✓ too many mediations where the participants just show up, not having allowed the mediator a chance to prepare;

- ✓ too many mediations where parties intentionally send client representatives with less than full authority to negotiate a settlement because, "if it's not going to work, why send our top decision makers?";

✓ too many mediations where the participants urge that a "joint session," a face to face encounter that is a hallmark of the process, be avoided; and

✓ too many mediations where the prospect of failure becomes a self-fulfilling prophecy; in other words, a "give up" attitude too often prevails.

Too often, these days, mediation has become an added layer of expense and delay in the process of litigating, a far cry from the noble objective of efficient and amicable dispute resolving. Too often lawyers figure out ways to manipulate the mediation process and use it for purposes that have nothing to do with dispute resolution.

Second Class Justice?

Mediation has also been challenged by those who believe the poor and disadvantaged are increasingly being diverted to "lower class justice" and discouraged from pursuing the quality of justice afforded only to those with the means to hire lawyers and litigate. Our obsession with "quantitative" results, our goal of moving cases through crowded courts, it is reasoned, is resulting in "qualitative" imbalances. Others have lodged concerns that our lust for dispute resolution through alternatives to litigation is a sign of inherent weaknesses in our society, if not a sign of moral decay. "(S)ettlement is a capitulation to the conditions of mass society and should be neither encouraged nor praised," wrote a distinguished Yale Law School professor.

But most of us are not law school academics. We have real problems in this real world that need resolution. Capitulation to the conditions of mass society is what we do when get up every day and fix breakfast, get the kids to school, and go to work. We don't have the time, money or appetite for disputing. First class or second class, we want justice we can afford. We need to move on.

The Great Philosopher

Yogi Berra, the baseball great, was once asked, "What time is it?" And he responded, "You mean now?"

Yogi also famously observed, "No one goes to that restaurant anymore—it's too crowded." My observations about recent developments in the practice of mediation may sound a similar note. If the use of mediation is so flawed, then why is the practice of mediation expanding and its overall popularity increasing?

Because it works. It is a bit like asking, "what's so great about being alive given that we have wars, and disease, and politicians?" The answer is: consider the alternative. Mediation works, but I think we can make the way we practice mediation better. Here's how.

All Together Now (Part III)

Years ago it was a standard practice at the outset of a mediation to convene the parties in a "joint session" or "joint caucus." The idea of skipping the joint session was pretty much unthinkable. The concept of creating a space and an opportunity for a dialogue has long been considered an integral part of the process, if not the key ingredient. Mediator training courses devote a substantial portion of the overall curriculum to the conduct of the joint session.

There have always been extreme circumstances in which the joint session is something to avoid. There have always been cases in which the mix of personalities and conflict will be too volatile, too emotional, and too polarizing, when merely putting the disputants in the same room could quickly escalate into something unfortunate, or at least be counterproductive. A case involving excessive use of force by a police officer, when the victim and the officer will be in attendance, is an example that comes to mind. The parent of a child who has been a victim of negligence or a crime will often have too much pain and rage to participate in a conversation with the other side.

But *even in such extreme circumstances* a joint meeting at a mediation can provide a unique moment, and opportunity, for the parties to come together and express their anger, frustration, hostility, and regret. So often the revealing of these human emotions is a critical step, a necessary step, in the psychology of resolution.

But in recent years the joint session has fallen out of favor with many. "It will be too emotional." "It will be too adversarial." As a mediator it is imperative that you listen to these sentiments. It is, after all, possible that they are correct. But as the mediator you should also ask more questions. What do you mean, "too emotional"? Does your client understand that a trial will be "too emotional," as well? Would it not help your client to be able to tell the other side, face to face, how angry and upset he is?

But to those who express this first category of objection my answer is as follows: I'm listening; I hear you; you may be correct; but let's at least explore the advantages of getting together with the other side despite your concerns.

A second category of objecting to the joint session is that it is simply unnecessary. "Will, a joint session will be a waste of time. We were in depositions with each other all last week and we know each other's case inside and out." Or how about this one, "Will, we agree with opposing counsel that we don't need a joint session. We both want you to just go back and forth a couple of times and then we'll know whether our case can be settled."

To me these heart-felt expressions reveal a forgotten sense of how mediation works, and the value of face-to-face communication. In a world in which the preferred means of communication is email, and not a meeting or even a phone conversation, are we not forgetting the power of human interaction? Would an advocate attending his or her first mediation be likely to suggest that a joint session will be a "waste of time," or is it more likely that the suggestion will come from someone attending their one hundredth mediation?

Human nature is such that the things we do repetitively become routinized; we become mechanical about them. A lawyer or client attending her hundredth mediation thinks she has "seen it all." To these participants, the process is scripted. "Just go back and forth a couple of times," means that in their experience, it seems that everything they learn at mediation can be gleaned in the first couple of moves. "We know each other's case inside and out" omits recognition of a substantial part of the value of the joint session, the human interaction part.

To those who express this second category of objection to getting together with the other side, I have a clear answer: you are wrong. Of course, I have a much friendlier way of saying it in person!

But many experienced and highly regarded mediators share the view that the joint session is too risky, and too often counter-productive. There are experienced mediators who, as a matter of policy, do not convene the parties in a joint session. I have listened to these experienced mediators explain that while they used to convene joint sessions routinely, they have reversed field and doubt that they will ever use a joint session again.

Which makes me wonder: how did we get to this point? How did we get from our perspective twenty years ago, when skipping a joint session was unthinkable and unheard of, to today, when many experienced participants routinely skip this step in the process?

I think I know the answer!

My perspective is that lawyers, over time, began to use the joint session in an overly adversarial and confrontational manner, posturing in front of the other side, and showing off for their own client. Threatening and criticizing your opponent can be a way of compensating for weaknesses in your position and your lack of preparation. If you have a strong position, why not lay out the facts and let the facts speak for themselves? One reason why joint sessions can become too adversarial is that lawyers make them too adversarial. One reason why joint sessions too often become emotional and confrontational is that the lawyers make them emotional and confrontational.

What is needed is more education, and a better understanding by the participants about how to effectively use the process, particularly the chance to dialogue face to face with the client on the other side of the table.

Which is another way of saying that what is needed is for more people to agree with me! Joint sessions are a good thing, when used correctly.

Let the Good Times Roll

A couple of years ago I convened a joint session, made my normal, brief remarks at the outset, and then turned it over to counsel for the Plaintiff. This experienced lawyer signaled to his assistant to dim the lights a bit in the conference room where we were all sitting, and then began a video projection on a large video screen at the opposite end of the table from the end where I was sitting. So far, so good. I enjoy a good movie as much as the next person.

"Good morning, everyone. Thank you for coming to the mediation." The lawyer, sitting immediately to my left but slightly turned and facing the screen like everyone else in the room, was the speaker in the video addressing the mediation participants! Let me repeat, we were watching in the video the man sitting immediately to my left! I don't know if there is a scientific or legal expression for "control freak," so as a trained professional neutral I will describe what I was witnessing as an obsessive attention to detail.

I simply could not believe what I was witnessing. I have noticed over the years the occasional effort of counsel to control the dynamics of the joint session by sticking very tightly to a prepared outline, or shutting the client off when the client wants to speak. Lawyers tend to not like things they cannot control. Lawyers tend to not like things that are spontaneous. So it is natural, in a sense, to expect from lawyers from time to time a reluctance to engage in a dynamic and open-ended conversation in a joint session. But to witness a lawyer presenting a video of himself prepared just for the occasion was, for me, over the top.

The irony, of sorts, in all of this is that dynamic and open-ended dialogue in a joint session more often than not sets the process on the right path. The point of mediation is communication and, through communication, the encouragement of evaluation and re-evaluation by the parties of their positions. At times I view the mediator's role as one of facilitating communication. The lawyers, it seems, too often view their role as one of limiting communication. Any barrier to communication, whether it is the reluctance to even convene in the same room as the opponent, sticking to a tight script or outline, or directing the client not to speak or ask questions, is a barrier to the effective use of the mediation process.

No Prep Is No Good

I remain fascinated by my experiences in recent years when mediation participants just show up at my office, having failed to communicate in any form or fashion anything about the case, leaving me clueless as we gather as to what kind of dispute I have in front of me. Lack of preparation did not happen when mediation first became popular, or it happened infrequently. But currently the failure of preparation happens far too often, clearly a symptom of the "too much mediation" syndrome.

It is easy to understand that everyone is busy, and that sometimes in the last minute crush of events the chance to send the mediator an email, briefly explaining what the case is about, the status of settlement negotiations, etc., just slips away. Besides, it is tempting if the lawyer and mediator are familiar with each other to think, "I'll just get to the mediation a few minutes early and visit with the mediator privately." Maybe this works out, but maybe it doesn't. Why do intelligent people, all of whom are desirous of resolving a dispute, go to the time, trouble and expense of scheduling a mediation, preferably with an experienced mediator, and then not allow the mediator an opportunity to use that experience to tailor the process to benefit them? It is not good advocacy on the part of counsel. Whether you are counsel or client, don't let this be you!

I Ain't Got Time for This: The "Half Day" Mediation Phenomenon

I began mediating disputes in the late 1980's. In the first few years I was rarely asked to schedule a mediation on a "half day" basis. I doubt that more than a half-dozen mediations were scheduled on a half day basis *in a year*. Most mediations, after all, were taking place as a result of a court order, and the order never referred to a limited or restricted time frame. Consequently, by implication or otherwise, the obligation to mediate was generally considered to be a "full day" obligation.

These days I average around three or four half-day mediations *each week*. What's happened? Have the rules changed? Have court orders changed? No. What has changed is how mediation is perceived, now that the participants have been to dozens, if not hundreds of mediations.

Not convinced? A few years ago I received a call from a couple of lawyers, on opposite of sides of a case I was to mediate a few days later. They explained, "Will, we're in a break in a deposition and we've been talking about our mediation coming up with you next Wednesday. We are on your calendar for a full day, but we agree that nothing ever happens until around 4:30 in the afternoon, so instead of coming to your office in the morning, could we just come around 2:00?" I know you are laughing but I haven't gotten to the funny part. The funny part is that they were not kidding.

So what is revealed in their call? To these lawyers the process of mediation had lost whatever drama it ever held for them. They had been to plenty of mediations in which seemingly "nothing happened" until the late afternoon; so the lesson they learned is that it is mysteriously just the positioning of the hands on a clock that reveals whether a settlement can be achieved.

These lawyers should have learned a different lesson, a lesson about the process and the steps that the participants must go through, but they learned something else. I suggested they just show up around 4:00 to achieve maximum efficiency!

In every Summer Olympics there are events in Track Cycling. In the Individual Men's Sprint in Track Cycling, two riders pair off in various heats on a severely banked, oval track. This event is, indeed, bizarre. For three laps the two riders crawl around the track, as slowly as possible. In fact, they are barely able to remain erect on their bicycles. The rider in front rarely takes his eyes off of his opponent, who stays a bicycle-length behind. But then, on the last lap, a bell is rung, all hell breaks loose, and the riders engage in a decisive sprint around the final banked turn to the finish line.

Perhaps the lawyers who wanted to come to the mediation at 2:00 had just seen this event at a recent Summer Olympic Games. The mediation process, to them, seemed to consist of agonizing slowness, before the real action on the final lap!

Indeed, "nothing really happens until the late afternoon" is a common sentiment and is based on actual experience. But the reasons for the phenomenon are known to mediators, and less often to others. The sentiment is also commonly expressed in the rationale given at the outset for scheduling the mediation on a half-day basis, "We've agreed that if our case can be settled, it can be settled in half a day"? If you catch yourself uttering these words, there is a decent chance that you are wrong, and here's why.

Many of us have had a car buying experience in which we agree with our spouse about how much of the family budget can be devoted to the new vehicle. Let's say that you and your spouse agree that after credit for the trade-in, you will absolutely, positively not spend a penny more than $15,000.00. The problem is that within minutes of arriving on the dealer's lot, it becomes obvious that there is one vehicle superior to all others: sunroof, leather, decent mileage, etc. (hereinafter, "The Car"). The Car, however, after the trade-in, costs $16,500.00. What do you do?

You do not immediately say, "ok". You look at other cars. You look some more. Sometimes you go to other dealers, or go home. But your mind never leaves The Car. You keep coming back to it. Hours go by. Finally, you and your spouse rationalize your decision to spend the extra money. After all, with monthly payments spread out for four years, it's only a little bit more each month. So then The Man takes you into the Little Room with the Little Table, and you start reviewing the paperwork, financing options, tax/title/license, service agreement options, etc. For some reason this always takes at least an hour, or two. Uh-oh. For you to drive The Car home, it's going to cost around $18,000.00. What do you do? Eventually, but not right away, you say, "ok". Why? *Because by now you are invested in the process of buying The Car.* You have invested your time (it's late in the day, and you need a new car), and you have definitely committed yourself emotionally to closing the deal.

If you and your spouse had agreed that morning, before you set out, that regardless of what you encountered, you would not allow the entire car buying experience to last more than four hours, you would never have completed the purchase.

Parties to a negotiation often have to walk up, or down, a *ladder of expectations.* This takes time.

A claimant in a personal injury matter has, for over two years, expected to realize at least $100,000.00 in compensation from a defendant. But after two hours of mediation, the claimant has been confronted with a new reality: despite the long-held expectation, his lawyer and the mediator seem to think the value of the case is only in the range of $50,000.00. The claimant processes this information, is at first resistant to it, but finally rationalizes until reaching a comfort level with the new potential recovery, and steps down the ladder. Three more hours go by. The claimant learns to deal with the depressing suggestion of the lawyer and mediator that the claim may, in fact, be worth only $35,000.00. The claimant takes another step. That evening, the case settles for around $20,000.00. This case would not have settled had a three or four hour time limit been imposed. Intellectually, it seems simple: just speed up the process and people will naturally make decisions in whatever time frame is allotted. No, they won't. It's not the way people work.

It is, of course, true that a half-day, or less, is appropriate for some cases. Courthouse "settlement week" programs, where cases are mediated at the courthouse by volunteers in only an hour or two, have been successful and popular for years. I know of one very fine, experienced and popular mediator in my hometown who schedules four or five, two-hour mediations each day, and even schedules them over breakfast, lunch or dinner!

This different perspective of advocates and neutrals is further revealed by a common experience of mediators: all of the participants, except the mediator, are completely surprised when a case settles. You, the mediator, are not at all surprised. Many experienced advocates simply do not understand how and why the process works. You, the experienced mediator, understand.

Ending on a High Note

I believe the reason why mediation has become popular and will continue to flourish, why it endures in the face of abuse and misuse by lawyers, over-dependence on mediation by Courts, and the ever-present symptoms of the "too much mediation" syndrome, is that it works.

You can make mediation work to your advantage. There are simple, mostly intuitive things that you can do to improve your overall experience with the process. The use of mediation is not going away. I wish you success.

Message Sent, Message Received

Some time ago I was mediating a "bad faith" dispute in connection with the handling of an insurance claim. In my state, as a result of a series of legislative amendments and appellate decisions, it has become more and more difficult for claimants to succeed on these claims. But a case involving a bad-faith insurance claim handling practice is ordinarily not any more difficult to resolve at mediation than most other cases.

The underlying dispute had to do with water damage to the insured's residence. Coverage was disputed. The homeowner's estimates for repairs, cost of alternative living arrangements during the repairs, and costs of storage of household items during the repairs, was around $90,000. The possibility of recovery of reasonable and necessary attorney's fees, allowed in my state, made the value of the claim a bit higher. The potential, however remote, for recovery of statutory treble-damages raised the value by another, slight increment.

After the joint session, I had a very appropriate private caucus with the homeowners, discussing their itemized damages so that I would be able to intelligently prod the insurer in the conference room down the hall. They appeared to be eager to settle. The water damage, regardless of whether the insurer would eventually be held responsible for it, was real, and it wasn't improving over time. Water penetration can lead to mold, and these homeowners were fearful of what might be happening behind the walls of their home. Without insurance proceeds, they did not have the money to make the necessary repairs. When I mentioned that a mediated settlement would probably mean they could get a check in fourteen days, if not sooner, they were practically on the edge of their seats. There had been no previous settlement discussions, or offers or demands, since the initial demand letter sent by their counsel. But the demand letter had been sent more than eighteen months before, so for negotiation purposes we were pretty much working with a clean slate. If ever there was a case that appeared to be poised for resolution, this was it!

I asked the homeowners' attorney if they would be willing to make an opening demand. They were prepared to do so. The attorney had done some Internet research and had determined that the net worth of the insurer was around $900 million. So $900 million became the client's opening demand.

Just when you think you've seen everything!

I was speechless. I looked at the homeowners. They just sat there, paralyzed.

I'm sure I mumbled something about how such a demand might jeopardize the opportunity to negotiate a compromise and resolution. The attorney pushed back. The insurer was in bad faith. The insurer had engaged in dilatory tactics and made pursuit of this claim exponentially more difficult than it should have been. The insurer was guilty of abusive conduct in discovery, which was the subject of a pending motion for sanctions. The insurer needed to understand that the homeowners meant business. "Will, get in there and tell them that our opening demand is $900 million!"

Your hunch about what happened next is correct. I made my way to the conference room where the insurance company representatives and counsel had been waiting for their turn to visit with me, communicated the demand of $900 million; everyone in the room burst out laughing, folded up their laptops and packed their briefcases, thanked me for my time, and walked out.

But that's not the funny part. After I reported to the claimant that the insurer had left, the claimant's attorney informed me that (a) mediation, in general, was a complete waste of time; (b) he had never experienced anything positive in a mediation; and (c) (this one kills me!) though he would never voluntarily participate in a mediation ever again, if required to do so by court order, he would do everything within his power to make certain that I was not the mediator!

We have ended with this heart-warming tale, which illustrates how mediations can fail, and how some reactions to the practice of mediation these days are not as positive as one might think. We can only pray that the homeowner's attorney reads this book, and as a consequence will forever after begin experiencing nothing but success in future mediations!